THE CARE OF FINE BOOKS

THE
CARE
OF
FINE
BOOKS

Jane Greenfield

Foreword by Nicholas A. Basbanes

Skyhorse Publishing

www.skyhorsepublishing.com

Library of Congress Cataloging-in-Publication Data
Greenfield, Jane.
    The care of fine books / Jane Greenfield.
    Introduction by Nicholas A. Basbanes.
    p. cm.
    Includes bibliographical references and index.
    Originally published: New York : N. Lyons Books, 1988.
ISBN-13: 978-1-60239-078-2 (alk. paper)
ISBN-10: 1-60239-078-9 (alk. paper)
    1. Books—Conservation and restoration.
2. Fine books. I. Title.
Z701.3.F53G73   2007
025.7—dc22
2007017618

10 9 8 7 6 5 4 3

Printed in Canada

CONTENTS

FOREWORD

By Nicholas A. Basbanes

What a delightful circumstance it is that in the early years of the twenty-first century we should have newly released a trusted compendium of bibliographic knowledge that is chock full of solid advice on the care and preservation of worthwhile books. Even more fortuitous is that it should be made available to a new wave of needy readers in a smart new edition. In just two short decades, *The Care of Fine Books* has achieved that most coveted status of all: It has become indispensable to collectors, librarians and booksellers, both professionals and amateurs alike, not only for the sound guidance it contains, but just as much for the grace and accessibility of its style and the directness of its writing. With so much information, entertainment, and instruction coming to us these days electronically in the form of zeroes and ones, it is reassuring to hear a voice call out for what amounts to caution and calm in the face of paradigm shifts of seismic proportions. That the voice is that of Jane Greenfield—a former conservator at Yale University who has spent a lifetime devoted to the making and the care of precious books—makes this new release all the more welcome.

The true beauty of it all is that this internationally respected authority on book conservation makes a distinction between volumes that are "rare" and volumes that are "fine," with the explicit understanding that all works set down on paper are important and worth saving in and of themselves. Fine books, Ms. Greenfield points out, "may be rare, but rare books are not always fine." What she is suggesting here, in essence, is that while scarcity and monetary value are certainly important factors to consider when deciding whether or not an artifact on paper merits protective measures, she also makes clear that something can be beautiful and important and well worth saving regardless of how many dollars it might fetch at auction or in the sales galleries of antiquarian booksellers.

Everyone knows, of course, that a First Folio of Shakespeare in great condition and with an impeccable provenance can command as much as $8 million in today's world, or that high spots in a genre we call "modern first editions"—a first issue copy of J. D. Salinger's *The Catcher in the Rye*, let's say, or Harper Lee's *To Kill a Mockingbird*—can secure sums of $25,000 or more, triple that for a fine copy of F. Scott Fitzgerald's *The Great Gatsby* with a crisp dust jacket. Needless to say, it behooves the keeper of such treasures to insure that they are treated properly and well, and the truth is that anyone who spends this kind of money on books of such stature does not need to be persuaded they require regular maintenance and close attention. It is all the other books in the bibliophilic universe—be they the "medium rare" tomes as some institutions now describe titles that occupy a kind of limbo zone between the commonplace and the scarce, or those that can be described simply as "fine"—that are the focus of her attention as well.

By Ms. Greenfield's definition, a "fine" book is a book that is printed on well-made paper, and bound "handsomely" in a way that the "mechanical components," as she puts it, "work well together." Mechanical components, of course, are quite different from the text, which is another consideration entirely, and a topic to consider elsewhere. In this instance, mechanical components are an aspect of aesthetics and involve elements of what are known as the book arts. By this measurement, the assumption is that books are important in and of themselves as expressions of human wisdom and inquiry, and like all other matters that are subjective and arbitrary, the appeal and relevance of the content is a personal matter. To her credit, Ms. Greenfield makes no distinction either between paperbacks and hardcovers; all books, in her benevolent view, are created equally, and all are deserving of long and fruitful lives.

The steps a careful custodian of books must take are laid out with great precision and admirable economy of words. And because she makes no assumptions on whatever prior knowledge a person might have on the architecture and framework of the miracle of human ingenuity we call a "book," she offers a concise refresher course on what constitutes its various parts and appendages, and outlines in specific detail the "factors," as she calls them, that affect books. They include light, temperature, humidity, and the weather most assuredly, but other threats such as babies, cats, rodents, mold, insects and the like are discussed in detail, too. She categories these as "biological attacks"—along with natural disasters that endanger these fragile objects on a daily basis; not surprisingly, "human error" is probably the most egregious menace of all. To protect against each of these perils, thankfully, there are steps to take, and they are outlined herewith in easy-to-master fashion.

And then there are the tidbits of advice that make perfect common sense, but need to be reiterated all the same. Do we need to be reminded that one must never "lean on a book" or to "use a book as a support" for writing? Or that it is not a very good idea to use a pen in close proximity to paper that is not intended to be marked permanently—ink spots are generally irreversible, after all, and pencils are so much cleaner to use—or that fingers and eyeglasses do not make for sensible bookmarks? The answer is yes indeed in each and every instance, since proper vigilance never takes a holiday.

There are those out there today who would regard the care of something so ubiquitous as the book as a decidedly quaint exercise, a medium of intellectual transmission that technology is sure to render irrelevant with time, and who consequently ask, why bother with such an anachronism? Never mind that the prediction of a "paperless society" has already been proven fallacious—offices use more paper today than ever before—or that books show no signs of forfeiting the hold they have on our psyches, our emotions, and our very well-being. It only makes sense that we pay these beloved companions the proper respect they have earned, for let it be said that no one individual ever really "owns" a book. The true bibliophile understands that we have a responsibility to watch over our books for a period of time, and then, when the time is right, take steps to insure safe passage to the next generation. With *The Care of Fine Books* at hand, the transfer can be made with ease, confidence, and a clear conscience that everything that could be done properly, has been done.

PREFACE

Fine books, that is books well printed on high quality paper and handsomely bound so that the mechanical components of the book work well together, are different from rare books since fine books may be rare, but rare books are not always fine. Rare books might be printed on newsprint, which contains damaging chemicals and has a short life expectancy (paperbacks and comic books, for example). Such books are rare because of their fragility and therefore scarcity.

Fine books stand a much better chance of survival than fragile, rare ones, but in both cases deterioration can be slowed (it can never be stopped completely) with proper housing and handling, and this is what this book is about. It is written for private collectors, rare book librarians, and curators, and ranges from simple handling procedures —how to pick up, or not pick up, a book—to optimum housing conditions and display techniques.

Knowing something about the materials books are made of, how they are put together, how they are affected by their environment, and what their most vulnerable parts are, helps in knowing how to store, handle and display them properly and the things to do, and not to do, to prolong their life and maintain them in good condition. The needless damage caused by improper handling is easily avoided.

A little over a hundred years ago William Blades wrote, in *The Enemies of Books*, "The surest way to preserve your books in health is to treat them as you would your own children, who are sure to sicken if confined in an atmosphere which is impure, too hot, too cold, too damp, or too dry." He also wrote the following, "I remember purchasing many years ago at a suburban book stall, a perfect copy of Moxon's Mechanic Exercises, now a scarce work. The volumes were uncut, and had the original marble covers. They looked so attractive in their old fashioned dress, that I at once determined to preserve it. My binder soon made for them a neat wooden box in the shape of a book, with morocco back properly lettered, where I trust the originals will be preserved from dust and injury for many a long year.

"Old covers, whether boards or paper, should always be retained if in any state approaching decency. A case, which can be embellished to any extent looks every whit as well upon the shelf! [sic] and gives even greater protection than binding. It has also this great advantage: it does not deprive your descendants of the opportunity of seeing for themselves exactly in what dress the book buyers of four centuries ago received their volumes." Conservation options today are ones which, according to Nicholas Pickwoad, Advisor to the National Trust for Book Conservation, "... require as little disturbance as possible" so it is reassuring that the opinion that judicious leaving alone is best was held so long ago by a man who gave serious thought to the well being of books.

Enough information on the guidelines and practices recommended by conservators for an interested reader to pursue this subject has been included, but has not been treated in any detail.

Information is listed under as many headings as possible for easy reference.

Products and publications mentioned in the text are listed in the chapter on Materials and Suppliers.

I would like to thank Suzanne Rutter, Technical Services Librarian at the Beinecke Rare Book and Manuscript Library and, particularly, Gay Walker, Preservation Librarian and Curator of the Arts of the Book in the Sterling

Memorial Library—both at Yale University; Kenneth Nesheim, appraisor; Mary Schlosser, collector; and Wayne Eley and Arthur Greenfield, who are neither librarians nor collectors.

New Haven, CT
August, 1988

THE CARE OF FINE BOOKS

The Nature of Books

The principal materials that make up books are as follows:

Papyrus	Cloth
Parchment	Vegetable fibers
Paper and paper	(thread and cord)
products	Plastic
Wood	Metals
Leather	Adhesives

Papyrus. The earliest inscribed papyri extant date from about 2500 B.C., but there is probably a long tradition of use behind them. It was the most common material used as a writing support throughout Egypt and the Greek and Roman empires and continued in use for documents in the Vatican as late as the eleventh century. High quality, newly made papyrus is white or cream color, flexible, strong, and very attractive.

Cyperus papyrus is a sedge plant which at one time grew abundantly in marshes along the Nile. Strips were cut or torn from the pith of its triangular stems and laid side by side on a hard, smooth surface so as neither to overlap nor leave a gap from shrinkage when drying. A second layer of strips was laid on the first, at a right angle to it. The two layers were then beaten and dried under pressure. The natural juices of the plant (polyesters) held them together. Although the plant grows to a height of seven to ten feet or more, the sheets made from it were not large, usually no more than eighteen inches high. They were pasted together to form rolls, which were later cut up to form codices. Although this seems an unusually roundabout means to an end, it allowed the scribe to choose his own page width. Papyrus was pasted together to stiffen covers or form book boards and for the manufacture of rope and candle wicks. We can only hope that it was uninscribed papyrus and not the tragedies of Euripides that burned quietly away of an evening in Gaul. It is said to have a very pleasant smell when burning. Papyrus has proved remarkably durable but is now brown and so fragile it is usually kept between sheets of glass or acrylic plastic. It becomes limp and molds if humidified so it is due to the dry climate of Egypt that the thousands of fragments and the books extant today have been preserved.

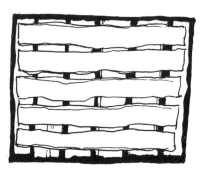

Papyrus structure

Parchment or vellum. These terms are generally used interchangeably—but precisely, parchment is split sheep, goat or other skin, and vellum is unsplit calfskin. In many cases it is difficult to tell them apart.

Vellum and parchment are made by liming a skin to remove the hair, repeatedly dampening and drying it under tension, splitting if required, scraping it smooth, and polishing. Fine vellum is extremely beautiful—white and almost translucent—a perfect surface for writing or painting. Parchment has been manufactured since at least 2000 B.C. in Egypt and since Roman times in Europe, but was almost entirely superseded by paper by the sixteenth century. It is only occasionally used today by calligraphers, conservators, or for fine binding.

Vellum is very durable but hygroscopic (that is, readily absorbs and retains moisture) and is subject to cockling, which is caused by changes in relative humidity. In the Mid-

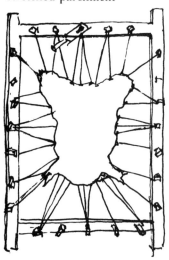

Stretched parchment

dle Ages and the Renaissance, books were bound in wooden boards with fastenings which held the vellum flat. Most of these fastenings have broken over time so protective containers are needed to hold the vellum flat today.

Paper. Although it is possible to make paper from almost any kind of fiber, it is largely produced from cellulose fibers. It is thought that, while competition with vellum lasted, a superior paper product was produced. Clean linen rags were bleached by the sun, pounded in stamping mills and formed into sheets with long interlocking fibers. Finally they were sized with gelatin, glue, or starch to prevent ink from spreading. The direction in which the fibers lie is called the grain, and paper folds more easily parallel to it. This is an important factor in making protective wrappers, etc. See Grain, page 108.

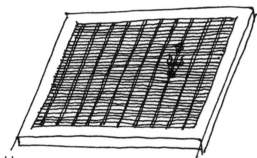

Paper mold

The process of paper making was invented in China in about 104 A.D. Knowledge of its manufacture travelled slowly from China by way of Samarkand, Baghdad, Damascus, Egypt and Fez, arriving at Jativa in Spain about 1150, Italy and further north shortly thereafter, and in America by 1690, when William Rittenhouse established a paper mill near Philadelphia.

Over the centuries, the history of paper has been one of decreasing quality to meet increasing demands, the nadir being around 1880 when mechanical wood pulp came into common use. This pulp has extremely short fibers and contains lignin and hemi-cellulose (amorphous polymeric substances related to cellulose), materials which break down into damaging compounds, producing a very fragile paper which usually discolors on exposure to light or air and becomes brittle. Although few fine books have been printed on wood pulp paper, many rare books (tracts, comic books, etc.) are printed on this kind of paper. Millions of books, published in the last half of the last century and the early years of this, are not expected to be usable by the year 2000.

Matters have improved in recent years. Research into the causes of the deterioration of paper, notably by William J. Barrow, has produced alkaline and permanent/durable papers and an awareness of the factors contributing to the degradation of cellulose. It has been determined that the pH (measurement of the hydrogen-ion concentration) should be 7 (neutral), or alkaline (7.1 to 8.5), that is, buffered against concentrations of acids. Many books now give the name and manufacturer of the paper used, with the statement "Acid free" or "This paper meets the requirements of the American National Standards Institute's Standard on the Permanence of Paper for Printed Library Materials ANSI Z39.48–1984," which does not tell the average person very much. However, paper which conforms to this standard's requirements for pH, alkaline reserve, folding endurance, tear resistance, and freedom from groundwood (mechanical wood pulp) is anticipated to last several hundred years. The mathematical symbol for infinity, ∞, may be added. This information is usually on the copyright page or in the colophon.

The various types of boards for book covers in use from the early sixteenth century—pasteboard, pulped paper boards and rope-fiber millboard—are all paper products and have lasted well.

Present day boards are made of wood pulp, waste paper, and other fibrous materials. They are not strong, and their longevity is uncertain. However, it is now possible to obtain acid-free boards which are used largely in fine hand binding. They can be specified if an important book is being rebound.

Wood. The word *codex* is, in fact, the Latin word for a plurality of wooden tablets. Wooden boards were used on books from very early times in Egypt into the sixteenth century in Europe. The most common woods were oak and beech. In America, thin oak or birch boards called "scab-

16

board," a contraction of scaleboard, which was a thin board used for hat boxes and by printers for justifying, were used in the eighteenth century.

Leather. The skins usually used for bookbinding are goat, calf, sheep, or pig, although deerskin, kangaroo skin, sealskin, human skin, and many others have occasionally been used. There are two ways of preparing skins for use —tanning and tawing. Vegetable tanning is the predomi-

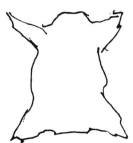

Animal skin

nant method of preparation. There is evidence that it was known in Egypt as early at 5000 B.C. It consists of liming a skin for ease of dehairing, soaking it in an infusion of a tannin-bearing plant such as oak bark or acacia, replacing the natural oils removed by tanning, dying, and treating it to produce different grains or surfaces. Tawed skins are prepared with a solution of alum and salt. They are remarkably durable and are usually white and often mistaken for vellum. If they are colored, the color remains on the surface of the skin. The most common dye used on alum tawed skin is kermes, made from the bodies of scale insects which feed on oak trees. The dye is a very bright pink. Pomegranate rind was also used as a dye for leather and produced a beautiful yellow.

Some early tanned leathers have proved remarkably durable, but by the eighteenth century increased demand caused a diminution in quality, as was the case with paper. Powdering leather and "red rot" due to faulty tanning and/or storage are frequent occurrences, usually accompanied by detached boards.

Cloth. Velvet, silk, satin, brocade, linen, canvas, and starch filled bookcloth, usually made of cotton, have all been, and still are, used for covering books. Cloth abrades easily and can be damaged by mold or wetting. Fine cloths were used for binding in the Middle Ages, sometimes as an additional cover added on top of a leather binding. Canvas came into limited use in England in the late eighteenth century, and cotton bookcloth, often with embossed grains, in the nineteenth. Since that time the quality of bookcloth has declined.

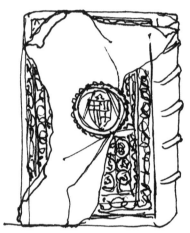

Cloth cover over leather

Vegetable fibers. Linen and silk have been used to sew the pages of books together, and linen or hemp cords have been used to support the sewing. If sewing supports are prominent on the spine of a book, they are called raised bands.

Synthetics. They have been used to sew books and as coverings. Their lasting qualities have not been established so this may be a problem for the owners and conservators of the future.

Metals and other materials. A variety of metals—gold, silver, brass, iron, and lead—have all been used for protective bosses, fastenings, chains, or decoration. Bone has been used to make the fastenings of Oriental bindings and ivory, cameos, *cloisonné* enamel, semi-precious stones, and egg-shells have also been used for decoration. They are the province of the museum curator so their treatment will not be considered here.

Adhesives. Animal glues, vegetable pastes, and synthetic adhesives are all used in binding books. Animal glues can cause a great deal of damage, often eating into the paper of the spine folds. Synthetic adhesives are not easily reversible. Vegetable pastes do not have the strength of the other two and are not flexible. Insects and rodents will eat both animal glue and pastes. Non-adhesive binding is an option to be considered whenever feasible.

The factors affecting books are as follows:

Light	Biological attack
Temperature	Human error
Relative humidity	Mutilation
Pollution	Disasters
Inherent vice	

All of these, except for inherent vice, can be controlled to a large extent by the collector or librarian.

Light. The most to least damaging light sources are sunlight, daylight, fluorescent light, and incandescent light, in that order. Exposure to light causes paper to yellow and become brittle and other book components to fade or discolor. Although all light is destructive, ultra-violet (UV) radiation with high energy and short wavelengths, particularly strong in sunlight and fluorescent light, is the most damaging. Unfortunately, the destructive action of UV radiation continues, although to a lesser degree, in the dark after exposure. It is irreversible. A weak light for a long period does as much damage as a strong one for a short period.

Temperature. Heat increases the rate at which chemicals, such as acids, attack books and causes a lowering of relative humidity (RH) which in turn causes the materials in books to contract. People are fond of saying that every 10°C the temperature is lowered doubles the life of the book. However, as 10 centigrade degrees equal approximately 18 Fahrenheit degrees, this is not very practical. If a book is brought from a very cold storage area to a warm reading room, condensation may form on the outside of the book. Excessive moisture in any form can be harmful. Fluctuations in temperature and relative humidity over a short period cause rapid, damaging, structural changes which are far more destructive than gradual seasonal changes.

Relative humidity. RH is the percentage of moisture in

the air at a given temperature relative to the maximum amount of moisture the air *could* hold at that temperature. Temperature and RH therefore interact closely. A low RH causes embrittlement and a high one provides receptive conditions for the formation of mold. Embrittled paper often breaks. In addition to staining, mold removes the size from paper and transforms it into a blotting paper-like substance with no strength at all. It can also cause pages to stick together irreversibly.

Pollution. Particulates and gaseous pollutants—sulphur dioxide, ozone, nitrogen dioxide, and chlorides—are ubiquitous. They interact with impurities in the books themselves and with unfavorable climatic conditions to degrade the components of books. They are unfortunately very hard to eliminate. Discoloration around the edges of pages is an obvious symptom.

Inherent vice. This is the term that conservators use for the impurities (and they are many) introduced into books during manufacture—such as ground wood fibers, alum rosin sizing and other acidic materials in paper, improper tanning of leather, and acidic adhesives or even sewing thread. The introduction of these damaging elements was at its height from about 1850 to 1900, with another peak during World War II. Faulty structure is also considered to be inherent vice.

Biological attack. Insects, dogs, babies, cats, rodents, and birds are all enemies of books. All of them except birds are apt to chew books, and saliva and chewing, in the case of dogs, can stick pages together, as can the excreta of insects. Insects eat paper, adhesives, wooden boards, and bindings.

The microbiological organisms of mold weaken the fiber components of paper and cause it to discolor and, in some cases, stick to its neighbor.

Human error and mutilation. Human error consists of improper storage and handling and mutilation is due to egotism.

Disasters. Fire, flood, and theft need not be defined.

BINDING STRUCTURE

The materials that books are made of and the factors that affect them have been described. The next few pages will show how books are put together, with emphasis on the two really important steps in binding—joining the pages of the text in sequential order and attaching a protective cover —along with a very brief outline of their history.

The roll was the predecessor of the codex (the manuscript book in the format we know today) and wooden tablets and parchment notebooks were its parents.

A roll was made up of sheets of papyrus pasted together, with the overlapping sheet to the left so that the pen would not catch at the join. The sheet is called *kollema* (plural, *kollemata*) and the join *kollesis* (plural, *kolleseis*).

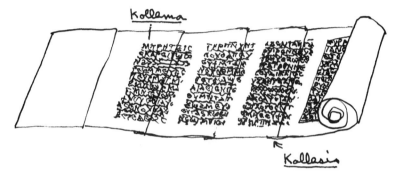

Roll, pen and pencase

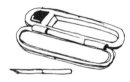

Average sheets were about 13″ × 9″ and an average roll somewhere between 24 and 35 feet long. A 35-foot roll could reasonably be expected to hold one of the longer gospels.

The horizontal fibers and the writing were on the inside, and a sheet with reversed fiber direction, the *protokollon*, began the roll. Another sheet and/or a wooden rod were sometimes at the end.

The title was at the end and perhaps written on a small label attached to one edge as well. The label was called a *syllabus*.

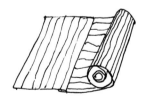

Protokollon

21

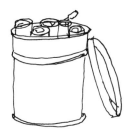

Capsa

Rolls were stored horizontally on shelves or vertically in a *capsa*.

The roll had the advantage of not needing binding to keep the text in order, although rolls were sometimes wrapped in a sheet of parchment for protection. However, it did have disadvantages: it had to be rewound by the reader or the next person to read it, it was usually written on one side only, reference was difficult, and it could become tangled if it were dropped.

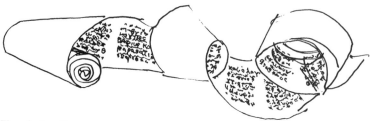

Tangled roll

A variant on the roll has been found in Britain. It was made up of thin, folded and hinged wooden leaves and was used for military records in the second century A.D.

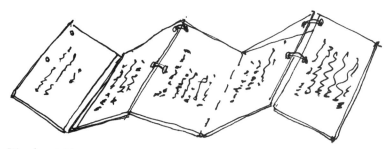

Wooden tablets

Wooden tablets consisting of up to ten leaves hinged together were used for ephemera—letters, accounts, school exercises, etc.—as early as the fourteenth century B.C., around the Mediterranean. They were left plain or whitened with gypsum to receive writing directly, or hollowed out and filled with wax and written on with the point of a stylus. The wax could be smoothed for reuse with the blunt end of the stylus.

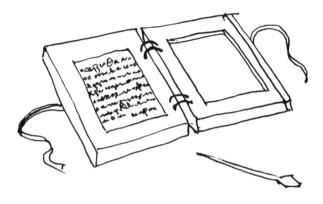

Tablet and stylus

Small parchment notebooks developed from tablets and were extensively used for accounts in Rome and the empire.

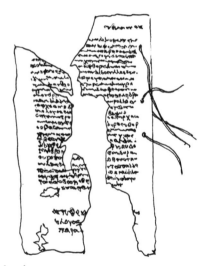

Parchment notebook

Readers have always felt strongly about the shape of their books. The most familiar shape is the only acceptable one, and resistance to a change in format has usually retarded its acceptance. It is not known just when the codex first came into use, but it was probably in the first century—B.C. or A.D. Although it had none of the disadvantages of the roll, the codex (papyrus or parchment) did not supersede it until the fourth century.

A folded section of a book is called a gathering, signature, or quire. Very early quire makeup has been deduced from the enormous number of fragments of codices, and sewing methods from occasional holes or pairs of holes in them. Scholars have tried to date these fragments in chronological order, but without any certainty, and their conclusions may have been skewed by the accident of survival as one eminent scholar has pointed out (E. G. Turner, *The Typology of the Early Codex*). In any case, dating seems to vary from scholar to scholar.

The earliest makeups were: Single bifolios; single sheets which could have been bifolios broken at the fold; single gathering of bifolios placed one within another. The single gathering seems to have been the most common, if not necessarily the earliest makeup.

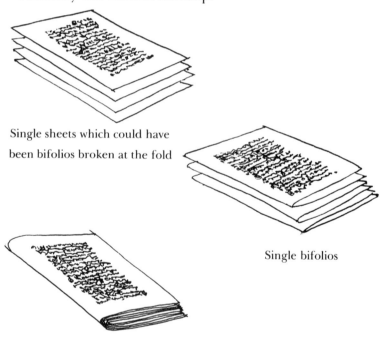

Single sheets which could have been bifolios broken at the fold

Single bifolios

Single gathering of bifolios placed one within another

All our knowledge of early binding comes from Egypt, so the early method is known as "Coptic" whether a bound manuscript is Coptic or Greek.

Single sheets or bifolios were stab sewn, probably loosely, as the writing often extended in beyond the sewing holes. There were no word breaks and very little punctuation.

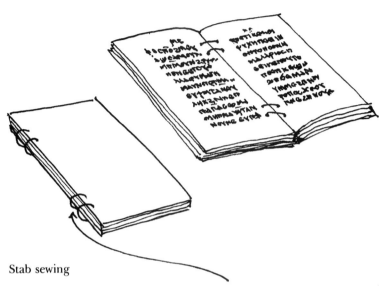

Stab sewing

Note the similarity of this sewing to the attachment of the wooden tablets and to present-day loose-leaf notebooks.

A single gathering could be sewn through the fold, making for much greater ease of opening. Leather or parchment stays were put under the twisted leather sewing thongs to protect the papyrus from abrasion. This method (without the stays) survives today in the form of stapled pamphlets. Sewing and the attachment of a cover were sometimes combined in one operation.

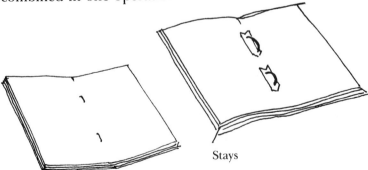

Stays

Stapled pamphlet

The leather thongs that held the gathering together were threaded through the cover and tied on the outside. Sometimes this process was reversed and the thongs were tied on the inside.

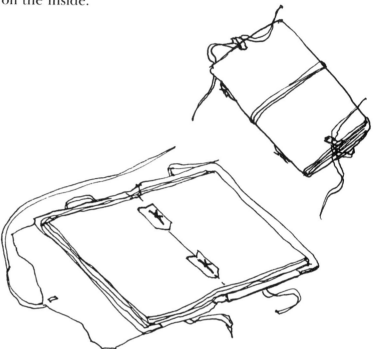

Sewing and attaching cover

Multiple quires were an improvement on a fat single one, as a quire could easily be added or subtracted (or reduced or enlarged) as needed, and the book opened better. Multiple quires were chain stitched, usually with two curved needles and two separate threads.

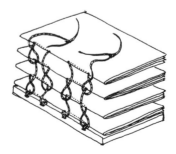

Chain stitching

Wooden boards, flush with the text block, were attached with the chain-stitch sewing.

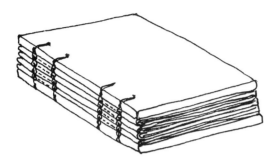

Chain stitching and board attachment

Headbands were also chain stitched and were laced into the boards, adding strength to their attachment.

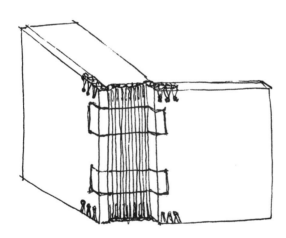

Headbands

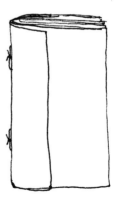

Spine linings, of leather, parchment, or cloth were used in some of these early bindings and extended to about one third the width of the book on either side of the spine.

A cover was made of leather stiffened with layers of papyrus pasted together, called cartonnage.

Spine lining

27

The spine lining, and perhaps a flyleaf, were glued to the cover and another layer of cartonnage was added. The leather was turned in on top of these layers, occasionally topped off with yet another flyleaf. Ties were added, usually of a different color from the cover itself, and designs were occasionally inked or drawn on the cover with a bone folder or similar tool.

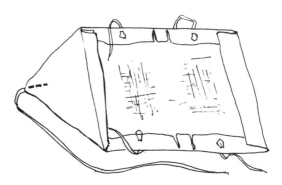

Cartonnage and ties

Boards were also attached in a separate operation. Thin strips of leather were laced through holes in the edges of the boards and adhered in grooves on the inside.

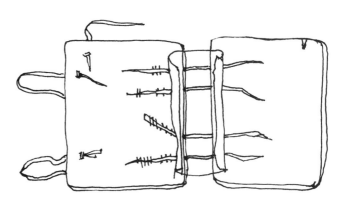

Board attachment

Vellum needed fastenings to keep it flat. These fastenings most certainly did so. This is C. T. Lamacraft's reconstruction of the binding of MS. Chester Beatty Coptic B, *Acts and St. John* (120 × 102 mm.), ca. A.D. 600 or earlier (Drawn from a photograph of a facsimile in the Library of the University of Michigan by T. C. Petersen).

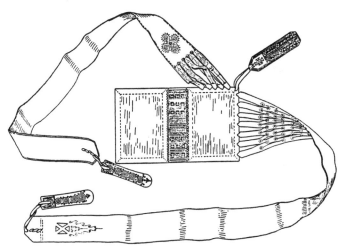

Reconstruction of MS Chester Beatty Coptic B

Coptic fastenings were varied and numerous—as many as nine might be found on one binding.

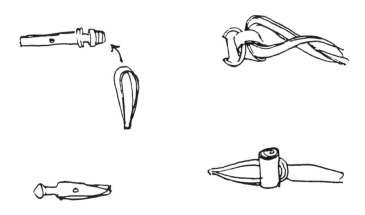

Coptic fastenings

War and the climate have destroyed early European bindings, but fifth-century mosaics in Ravenna and paintings in the catacombs in Rome show bindings like this, stab sewn and sewn through the fold.

430–450A.D.

422–432 A.D.

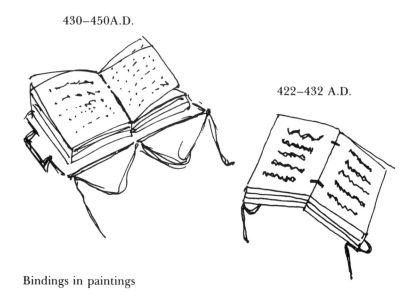

Bindings in paintings

The tiny (5.3″ × 3.6″) Stonyhurst Gospel of Saint John is the earliest European binding to survive. The structure closely resembles Coptic ones with chain-stitch sewing and the same kind of board attachment. It was bound for Saint Cuthbert late in the seventh century. It is interesting to note that the Archbishop of Canterbury at the time was Greek and the Abbot of Saint Augustine's in Canterbury was an "African." These princes of the church may possibly have had Coptic binders in their retinue.

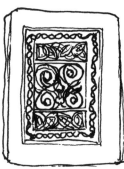

Stonyhurst Gospel

Heavy boards and bookblocks required sewing stronger than chain stitching and a sturdier board attachment. Sewing on supports—thongs, bands, cords, or straps—provided this. The Victor Codex belonging to Saint Boniface, who was martyred in 754, is the earliest surviving example of this sewing.

This is the path of the sewing thread—inside the fold of each quire, out around the supports, and back into the quire again.

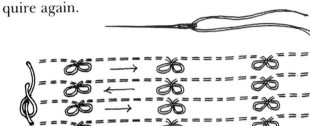

Sewing on supports

Thread was wound around the supports between going out of and into the quires so that the supports were completely wrapped on the spine.

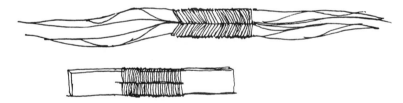

Thong and slit strap supports

Headbands sewn at the head and tail added decoration as well as strength.

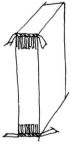

Headband patterns

From the seventh through the twelfth century many books had tabs at each end of the spine, presumably to make it easier to take them out of the chests in which they were stored.

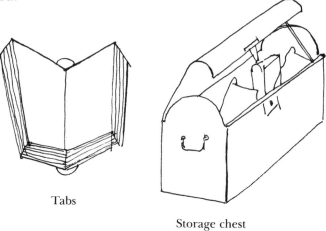

Tabs

Storage chest

Books were also stored in presses (bookcases), with the title sometimes written on the tail or fore edge.

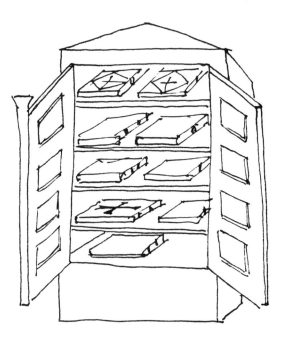

Book press

Binders tried many ways of attaching the sewing supports into the boards, evidently not realizing that the most vulnerable part of a binding is in the joint, where the opening and closing of the board weakens the sewing support.

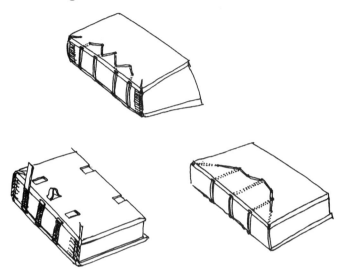

Attaching boards

Edges were trimmed, often far too much, with shears, a chisel, or an unusual implement called a plow.

Up until about the eleventh century, monasteries provided the greatest part of the reading public. Monastic bindings were usually plain. Binding met the needs of the user—and the size of his purse.

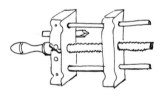

Plow

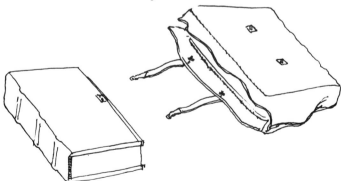

Monastic bindings

This plain, eleventh-century binding was sewn to a spine lining and held in an outer case by the turn-ins which were folded around the lining and headcap cores.

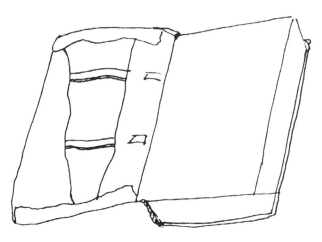

Eleventh-century vellum binding

At left is a fifteenth-century girdle book, perhaps used by a traveller. The knot was passed under the belt and, as the book was upside down in the wrapper, it could be lifted and read without detaching it.

This fifteenth-century book was sewn and attached to the vellum case in one operation—a relatively quick, inexpensive way to bind.

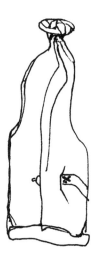

Girdle book

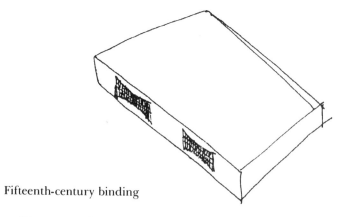

Fifteenth-century binding

However, there was never a time when bindings were not decorated.

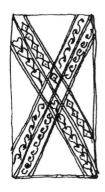

Egypt, 4th century

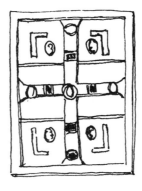

Italy, 7th century

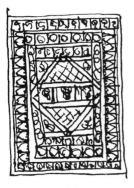

England, 11th century

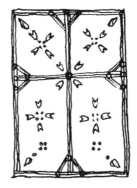

France, 12th century

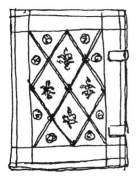

Germany, 15th century

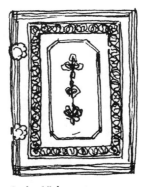

Italy, 15th century

The last step in binding was attaching the fastenings. There were two kinds: strap and pin, and clasp and catch. The straps were often of a contrasting color and the clasps and catches were decorative.

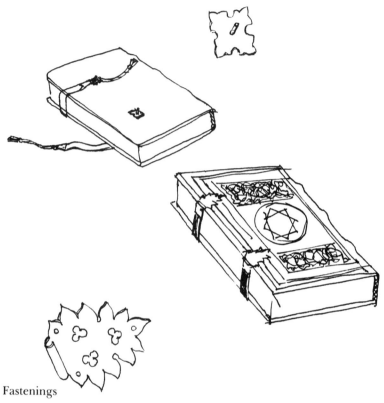

Fastenings

Metal bosses and fittings to save the cover from abrasion were also popular and a design element.

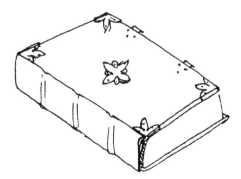

Fittings

The demand from schools in the twelfth century, the universities in the thirteenth, and printing in the fifteenth, increased book production immeasurably. The stationer, precursor of the publisher and bookseller, entered the picture. Quicker ways of binding began to evolve.

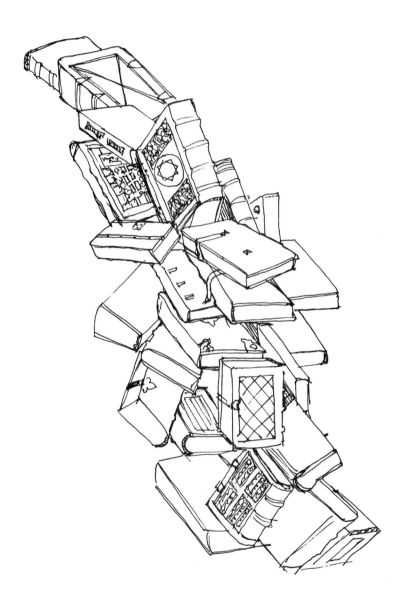

In the sixteenth century, paper almost entirely replaced vellum.

A full sheet of paper could be printed and folded to make a quire of a certain number of pages, depending on how it was printed.

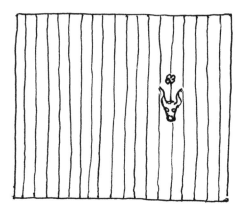

Full sheet

The size of a common sheet of printing paper ranged from about 15″ × 12½″ to 28″ × 23″.

One fold: 2 leaves, 4 pages. *Folio.*
Two folds: 4 leaves, 8 pages. *Quarto.*
Three folds: 8 leaves, 16 pages. *Octavo.*

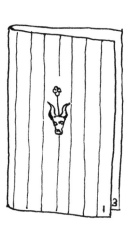

Folio

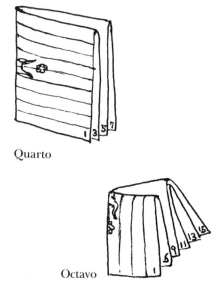

Quarto

Octavo

The use of paper caused changes in binding structure. There is not as much air between sheets of paper as there is between sheet of vellum, particularly as the paper quires were beaten to consolidate them. This meant that the sewing threads caused swelling at the spine of paper books.

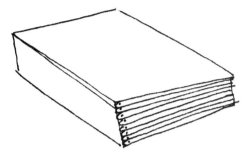

Swelling caused by sewing

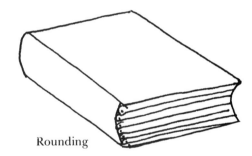

Rounding

Rounding the spine slightly cut down on the swelling.

The backs of the quires were fanned out. This did away with the rest of the swelling caused by the sewing threads and provided a shoulder against which the boards could fit.

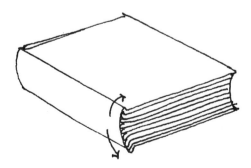

Backing

Wooden boards and fastenings were not needed to keep the paper flat, as was the case with vellum, so boards made of sheets of paper pasted together replaced wooden ones. These pasteboards were, of course, much thinner than wooden ones and did not require time-consuming shaping.

Sewing supports were often single instead of double thongs as pasteboards were not heavy. Ribbon ties replaced the earlier fastenings and then disappeared altogether.

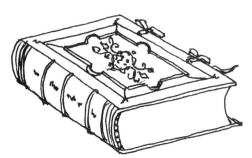

Ribbon ties

Book structure changed very little in the seventeenth and eighteenth centuries. The most important innovation in decoration was titling on the spine, although not all books were titled.

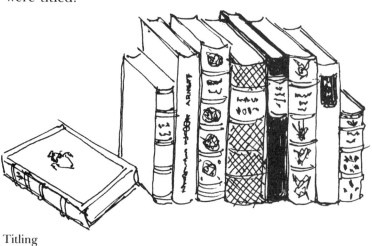

Titling

Paper cases, called binding "*alla rustica,*" were used in the eighteenth and nineteenth centuries and have proved very durable. Today, vellum or paper cases, without adhesive, are used as conservation bindings.

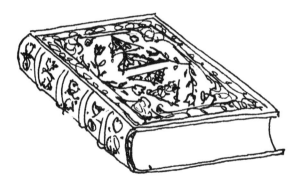

England, 17th century

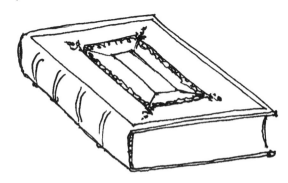

America, 18th century

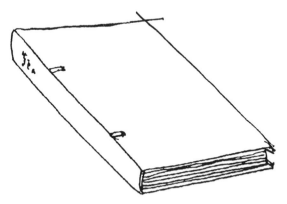

Paper case "alla rustica"

In the eighteenth century decoration went from elegant simplicity to bindings with no inch left undecorated, and back to comparatively plain designs, often by eminent artists. Cloth for covering became the norm.

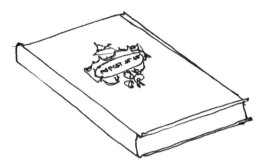

Paper binding, England, 1830

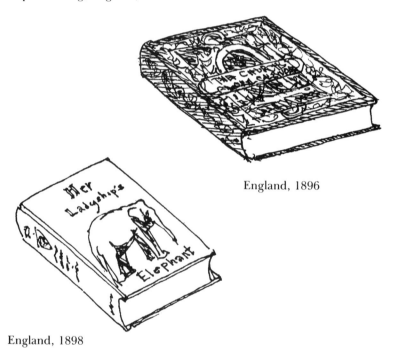

England, 1896

England, 1898

In the nineteenth century binding gradually became mechanized to meet the demands of increased literacy. Case binding replaced earlier structures. A case binding is the one we know today. The book is forwarded—that is sewn, endleaves added, trimmed, rounded and backed, and the spine lined.

The book is then ready to be cased. The case is made separately and the book is glued into it.

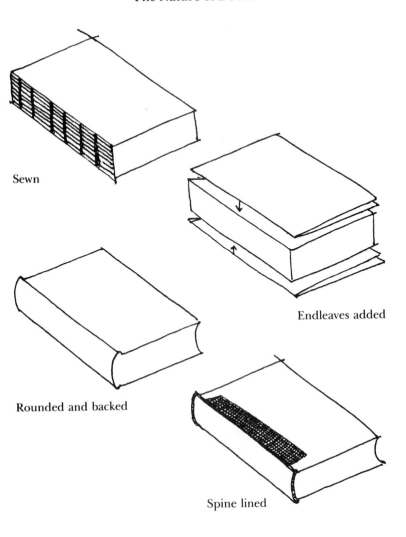

Sewn

Endleaves added

Rounded and backed

Spine lined

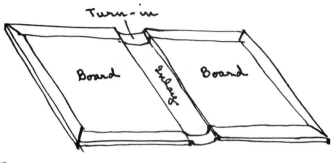

Case

While traditional methods of binding continue to be used, adhesive binding, which had been tried unsuccessfully in the eighteenth and nineteenth centuries, is very common today and could be considered the one innovation of the twentieth century.

The average paperback has to be held open by force because a stiff cover is glued to the spine. However, some adhesive bindings open well and, as adhesives improve, this type of binding may become an acceptable binding method —or will if the adhesives hold. Adhesive binding has the advantage that a double spread can be seen without the distraction of sewing thread in the fold.

However, today's finest books are still sewn through the fold.

Paperback

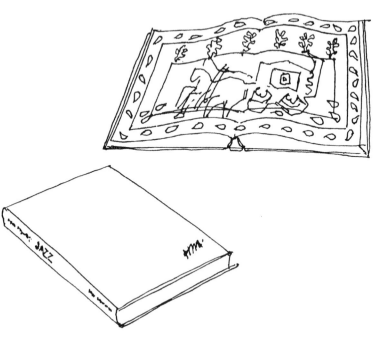

Adhesive binding

The Parts of the Book

Terminology used by bookbinders.

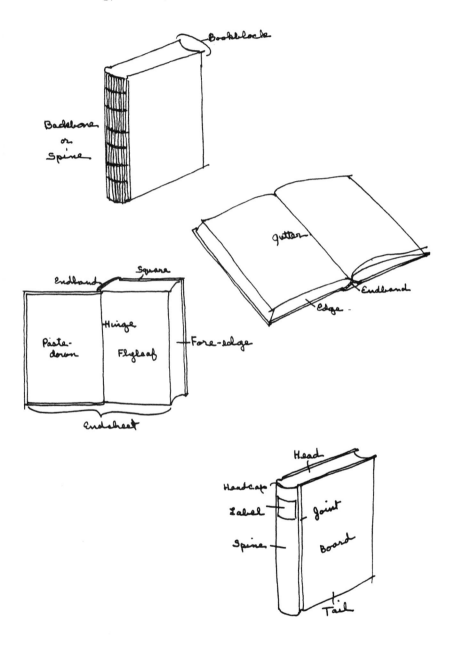

Bookblock

Backbone or Spine

Gutter

Endband

Edge

Endband

Square

Paste-down

Hinge

Flyleaf

Fore-edge

Endsheet

Head

Headcap

Label

Joint

Spine

Board

Tail

The Storage of Books

Books should never be housed in the attic, cellar, or barn.
This seems like an absurd statement, but all three areas
have been used, sometimes with disastrous results. The dan-
gers of storing books in these places are varied. An attic or
top floor is usually hot and dry and this can cause embrittlement. Damage from the *heat* of a fire is greatest at the
top of a building. Areas below ground level are subject to
flooding. They are usually dark and humid and so can attract insects and rodents. Barns (people have been known
to store books—even rare ones—in barns) can also harbor
insects and rodents, and, having no climate control at all,
can cause books to mold or become brittle.

Desirable general conditions

The storage area should be weatherproof, insect and animal proof as far as is possible, secure as far as is possible,
easy to clean, and have a floor strong enough to support at
least 350 lbs. per square foot.

It should have as close to a perfect climate as possible,
controlled lighting, and adequate space for processing.

The following form was designed by Gay Walker and
me in connection with a collection-condition survey. Although it was designed for large, circulating libraries, and
although some of it is not pertinent to rare book libraries
or private collections, it does pinpoint the factors that should
be considered in assessing their environment.

ENVIRONMENTAL SURVEY

Library:_____ Address_____

Date built:_____ Date/s remodelled:_____

Condition:_____

_____

Materials of walls:_____ of roofs:_____

Position of library within the building:_____

No. of floors:_____

Windows in stack areas: Sealed?_____ Screened?_____

Square footage underground:_____

Location of materials requiring special handling:_____

_____

Location of rare or unique materials:_____

_____

Climate

Local outside Environmental Protection Dept. pollution levels:_____

Temperature range:_____ R/H range:_____

Controls: When on:_____ When off:_____

   Heating, type:_____

   Air conditioning:_____

   Air filtration:_____

   R/H control:_____

Artificial lighting, type:_____ UV filters:_____

   Automatic timers:_____

Sunlight: Stack exposure:_____ Location:_____

Exhibition case climate:_____Controls:_____

Fire Prevention Measures

Monitoring equipment, types:_____

Automatic extinguishers:_____*Portable extinguishers:_____

   Checked regularly:_____

The Storage of Books

Flood Control

*Position of potentially damaging water and steam pipes:_____

_____

*Position of drains:_____

*Location of turn-off valves:_____*Electrical outlets:_____

Security

Building alarm systems, types:_____

Open stacks:_____ Closed stacks:_____

Book alarm systems:_____

Biological Problems

Evidence of insect activity:_____

Evidence of animal activity:_____

Evidence of fungus:_____

Shelving

Exposed bolts:_____ Sharp edges:_____

Mis-shelving problems:_____

Types of book supports:_____ Used?_____

Housekeeping

Materials used:_____

Regular cleaning of floors:_____ Books:_____

History of Environmental Problems

Fire:_____

Water:_____

Light damage:_____

Biological attack:_____

Security problems:_____

_____
*Mark on a floor plan.

Knowing the answers to these questions, and having a floor plan marked as suggested on the form, are a good foundation for providing proper housing for your books.

The next three sections—on Light, Temperature and Relative Humidity—will describe the climatic conditions considered optimum today, how to achieve them or something close to them, and the monitors available for them.

With one or two exceptions, rare book libraries are part of larger research libraries, and climate control on a large scale is handled from a central plant and not by the rare-book section itself. However, it is advisable for both librarians and private collectors to know what climate is needed for the well-being of books.

Garry Thomson, in *The Museum Environment*, has said that we need not, indeed cannot, be highly accurate in our climate control. We can, however, try to keep within the limits stated below. *Remember that avoidance of extremes is the most important factor in providing a good environment for books.*

Light

In general, light (visible radiation) levels should be kept below 200 lux and UV radiation below 75 lux. Remember that the damage caused by UV radiation continues to a lesser degree even when the source is removed. Objects on exhibition require a very low light levels, and it is surprising how easily the eye adjusts to low light. See Display, pages 126-27.

Direct sunlight. This is very strong in UV radiation. Sunlight and daylight are easily shut out by painting over skylights or windows, installing UV filtering film, or installing opaque curtains in storage areas and curtains or Venetian blinds in public rooms or in private collections. Curtains or blinds should be kept closed when rooms are not in use.

Acrylic sheets, such as Plexiglas UF-3 and Acrylite OP-2, can be used to filter out UV radiation. These sheets are ⅛" or ¼" thick and can be cut to your specifications from large sheets which are 48" by 96". UV filtering films or varnishes are also available but are apt to bubble and are not long lived. They should be installed by the distributor. These materials easily collect electrostatic charges so will need frequent dusting. Acrylic sheets should be checked with a UV meter after ten years, the films and varnishes after five.

Fluorescent light. The advantages of fluorescent light are that it is cheap and generates very little heat. It is high in UV radiation, but UV filtering sleeves are available that slip onto fluorescent bulbs. Contrary to most belief, these sleeves lose little or no effectiveness with age.

Incandescent light. This is the least damaging, and is the best light for books. It emits more heat than fluorescent light so, within reason, the light source should not be too close to the book.

Turn lights off whenever they are not needed.

Light monitors. The terminology of light measurement is somewhat complicated—as is light itself for that matter. An illuminance value of one lux equals one lumen per square meter. Lumen is the radiant energy flux as perceived by the human eye. One lux equals $\frac{1}{10}$ of a footcandle. Light monitors may give readings in any one of these terms.

An illuminance level meter is available which measures light in footcandles. A 50 lux (5 footcandles) level for exhibition and storage is recommended. A higher level would be preferable for study.

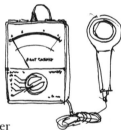

Illuminance level meter

The Canadian Conservation Institute has developed a light-damage calculator that is inexpensive and should prove very useful.

There are also instruments to measure UV radiation. Monitors should be held beside the book, facing the light source to read the light or radiation falling on the book,

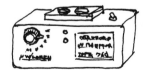

UV monitor

not that reflected from it.

Blue scales. These are cards with strips of blue wool cloth, which fade at different rates, pasted on them.

Tape a card to a stiff piece of cardboard with double-faced tape and tape a strip of black paper or other opaque material around it, leaving half exposed. The cardboard holds the blue wool card rigid so that the light will not seep under the opaque shield. Write the date of installation on the back of the card and position it beside the object to be monitored, facing the light source.

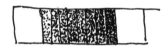

Blue scale card

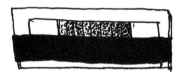

Half of card masked

Check the card at two-week intervals. Evidence of fading will show up very quickly.

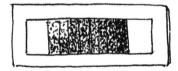

Evidence of fading

Being able to demonstrate that fading is taking place is often enough to generate immediate action—the installation of a curtain or the removal of an object from exhibition for example.

Temperature

A temperature between 60°F and 70°F (the closer to 60°F the better) is considered best for books.

As already mentioned, keep books away from radiators or other heat sources. Install air-conditioning if possible.

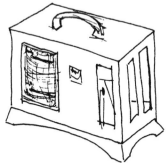

Hygrothermograph

Temperature monitors. There has been a great proliferation of climate monitors in recent years. The names of these instruments vary from manufacturer to manufacturer, but one can assume that any word with hygro (Greek: wet, moist) and therm (Greek: hot, heat) in it, in any combination, relates to temperature/RH monitors or recorders.

Obviously, a thermometer is the simplest monitor for temperature alone. However, there are small thermo-hygrometers, suitable for use in exhibition cases, which monitor temperature and RH, and hygrothermographs which *record* temperature and RH on a seven-day chart.

Thermo-hygrometer

Hygrothermographs must be regularly calibrated and the ink replaced when necessary. There are various instruments for calibrating hygrothermographs, a psychron being a fairly simple one to use.

A high-low thermometer is useful if a record is kept over a long period and checked at the same time of day.

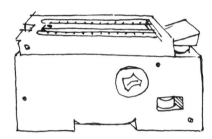

Psychron

Relative humidity

Controlled humidity is the most important factor in providing a proper environment for books.

For many years a RH of between 45% and 60% has been recommended for books. However, the dry sands of Egypt have preserved third- and fourth-century papyrus and vellum books, and the dry coastal plain of Peru has preserved many objects—among them mummies and cloth—which are of similar materials, so close to the lower end of the scale may be best. Also, dyes fade more rapidly at a high RH. The best climate control is a central air-conditioning system that regulates both temperature and RH. It is very expensive, requires constant monitoring (as does all machinery), and is outside the scope of this book. Anyone interested in such a system should read *The Museum Environment* by Garry Thomson before starting discussions with architects and engineers.

Short of such a system, window air-conditioning units, fans, humidifiers, and dehumidifiers will help maintain a climate within the limits outlined above (60–70°F temperature, and 45% to 60% RH).

Fans. Fans will help prevent formation of mold in humid summer weather. Fans are also useful in dealing with the aftermath of floods. Very small, fairly quiet fans are now available to keep air moving.

Except in heavily polluted areas, opening windows to allow air circulation on dry, breezy days is also helpful. Thomson has put it very well, "...some good and little harm can come from judiciously opening windows onto good weather."

Dehumidifiers. Humidity in summer can be very high. There are two types of dehumidifier: dessicant, suitable for cool climates, and refrigerant for warm ones. Unless dehumidifiers are vented to the outside they must be emptied by hand, the frequency depending on the amount of water taken in. This can be every day in some areas.

For enclosed areas such as exhibition cases, safes, or closed shelving, silica gel, a dessicant which can absorb 40% of its weight in water, can be used. Blue indicating silica gel turns pink when saturated. It can be dried out at 300°F and reused, and is usually packaged in oven-safe containers.

Humidifiers. Humidification is needed as much in winter as dehumidification is needed in summer in climates where buildings must be heated.

Atomizing humidifiers put water, and the minerals it contains, into the air, so within a few months a gray deposit may start to form on the objects in the room. However, demineralizing cartridges, a water-treatment liquid which precipitates solids, and tank cleaners can minimize this problem.

Evaporative-type humidifiers are preferable as they soak up water in a sponge and then blow the air through it. The sponge must be washed about once a month to remove the mineral scale left on it (but not on the books) by the evaporating water.

Relative humidity monitors. In addition to the instruments mentioned above, there are humidity-indicating cards with patches labelled with RH in 10% steps. Their color ranges from pink at the dry end to blue at the wet one. The RH is read at the point of change between pink and blue (presumably lavender). These cards are not terribly accurate, but should give adequate warning if humidity is approaching a dangerous level. These cards can be put on

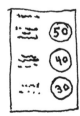

Humidity indicating card

shelves, in exhibition cases, and in various spots in a room to locate pockets of humid air, or can be used as general monitors. The colors do not reverse.

Inexpensive thermometer/hygrometers, although not very accurate, are also useful general indicators.

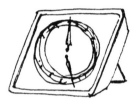

Thermometer/hygrometer

The Aqua-Boy. This is an instrument that can be used for measuring the moisture content of paper. Heads with flat, different length prongs are available. After sliding the prongs in the book, put a weight on it and read the moisture content. As readings vary with the amount of pressure, this will give you relative indications, if not absolutely accurate ones.

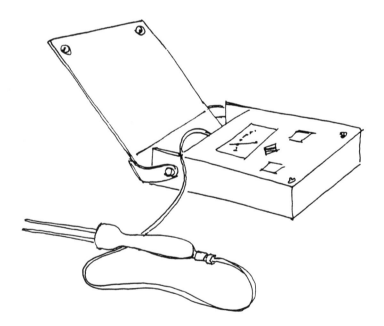

Aqua-boy

Opening a book and pressing the page at the opening against your cheek (if you are not wearing cosmetics) can tell whether or not a book is damp. If the paper feels cold, it is damp. This is the way mothers usually check babies' clothes to be sure they are dry.

Pollution

Complete removal of pollutants requires a ducted air-conditioning system with appropriate filters. Room air cleaners are available which include filters containing combinations of synthetic fibers and fiberglass for particulates and activated carbon filters for gaseous pollutants.

Do not allow smoking near books. It is a fire hazard, and the smoke is a pollutant.

Do not use electrostatic precipitators (electro-filters) to cut down on dust as they produce damaging ozone, and help convert sulphur dioxide to damaging sulphuric acid.

Provide protective enclosures, at least for the rarest items in the collection. Items protected this way will be less affected by ambient pollution.

Pollution monitors. Measuring pollutants, whether particulate or gaseous, is not easy. The environmental protection Department, listed in the section on state government in the telephone book, can give information on local levels of pollution, but it is simplest to assume that it exists in your library or home. Levels are, of course, highest in urban and nearby areas, and the levels indoors are roughly half those outdoors.

In addition to a controlled climate, books need spacious surroundings and specialized furniture.

Processing area.

This is helpful for a private collection and vital for a library. It should naturally be commensurate with the size of the collection. There should be:
- Adequate shelving for necessary reference books and an average number of books to be processed at one time. There should be some shelving for oversize books so that they will not take up space on work tables.
- Storage space for the materials needed in processing

—bookplates, flags, materials for protective wrappers (see page 111), leather dressing and adhesives, waste sheets, and rags. None of the above takes up much space except for the materials required for protective wrappers.

• Cataloging is presumably done elsewhere in a library, but a private collector may want a personal computer for record keeping and cataloging.

• A work table to work on and another for temporary storage—such as overnight storage after oiling, for example.

• A surface to paste on, 14″ × 18″ or more, of marble or formica or a lithographic stone.

• A book truck.

Several tables are preferable if a large number of books are to be processed. Work should be done in a place set aside for that purpose, not in one already in use for something else.

There should be enough space around work tables for book trucks or passersby to move without brushing books off onto the floor.

Umbrellas or wet clothing should not be allowed in the work area.

Bookshelves

Bookshelves should be sturdy enough to take the weight of the books without sagging, with upright supports at least every 36″. They should be adjustable and easily cleaned, with adequate support or packing at the ends and at least 1″ of air space above the tallest book. There should not be any rough edges or sharp protrusions. Except at the ends, they should be as open as possible to permit maximum air circulation, although in heavily polluted areas, closed backs and glass fronts are best. Closed cases are also a protection, to some extent, from fire. The area below the bottom shelf should be at least 6″ up from the floor to allow a vacuum cleaner nozzle or broom to reach underneath it, to prevent dust from accumulating on the books near the floor, and to avoid water damage should there be a problem.

Kickstools and ladders. Kickstools or ladders should be provided for tall bookshelves.

Bookshelves, location. Shelves should be located away from heat sources. In addition to the damage from heat itself, rising air from radiators will deposit dust. Preferably, shelves should not be along an outer wall which may be damp or might collect condensation. If they must be positioned there, an inch of free space should be left between them and the wall. They should not be positioned directly under water or steam pipes or so that direct outdoor light falls on the books. Freestanding shelves, although not always practicable, allow increased air circulation.

Bookshelves, wooden. Wooden shelves almost always have a mechanism for adjusting them. This can be two metal uprights with holes for clips or holes for wooden pegs at 1″ intervals in the ends of the shelves. There should be distinctive hanger holes at intervals to help in getting shelves level. In most commercially produced shelving, the shelves are grooved underneath to accommodate the pegs or clips. If this is not the case, or if the pegs protrude partially as they usually do, the books at the ends should not be so tall that the clips or pegs can abrade them. In existing shelving, a barrier of wood or other rigid material may need to be placed between the metal uprights and the adjacent book, as the uprights are not usually inset in the ends of the bookcases. An inch of space between the back of a case and the shelves helps air circulation.

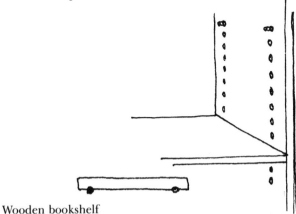

Wooden bookshelf

Bookcases with glass fronts hinged at the top. The opening mechanism of old-fashioned bookcases like this can damage the heads of books, so only short ones should be stored in them. However, new ones of the same type do not have the damaging opening mechanism.

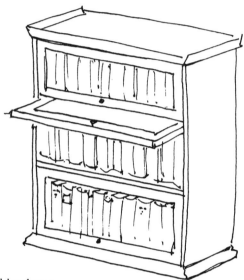

Glass-fronted bookcase

Bookcases, open end. They should also have a rigid support added at each end as otherwise part of the book stored at the end will, in due course, bulge out and the book will become deformed, probably permanently.

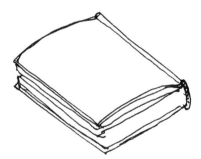

Result of open-end shelving

Bookshelves, finishing. There are two schools of thought on this subject. One holds that untreated wood helps to stabilize the relative humidity and is therefore to be recommended, and the other believes that unsealed wood and some finishes emit harmful vapors. This theory does not explain why the unsealed oak or beech boards of fifteenth-century books have not visibly affected the books adversely. However, untreated wood is not very practical, particularly as it is hard to keep clean. Commercial shelving with a baked-on finish can be used, or, if you are having shelves made, use solvent-based acrylic paint or solvent-based acrylic varnish to finish them. Use a primer and two or three coats of paint or varnish, covering all areas of the shelving including the ends of the boards. Allow the finish to dry thoroughly before shelving books.

Bookshelves, metal. Adjustable metal shelving with proper supports at the ends, open at the back, and with a baked-on finish is also available. These finishes are now in question, but custom made museum storage systems are now available. See page 145. The area below the bottom shelf is usually closed in with a strip of metal. Insects and dirt collect in this area, and the strips must be removed in order to mop up the water in the case of a flood. It is best to have the area under the bottom shelf open. The only disadvantage of metal shelving (which does not outweigh its good points) is that condensation can form on it. However, this is only under adverse climatic conditions. Climate control is the obvious solution.

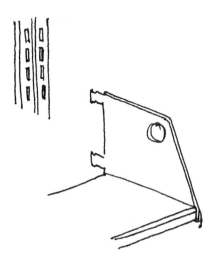

Metal bookshelf

Bookends

Various types of bookends are available. Hanging bookends made of metal tubing, which require tracks underneath the shelving, are not satisfactory, nor are standing bookends, even if care is used to slide them gently under the books.

A metal file box, 8¼″ × 5″ × 5¾″, filled with shot or pennies makes a good bookend for medium size books. It avoids the abrasion possible with stands that are slid under books.

A smooth wooden block, about 4″ thick and 10″ square, makes an excellent bookend. Holes can be bored in the base and filled with weights which can be sealed in. This will probably require the services of a carpenter.

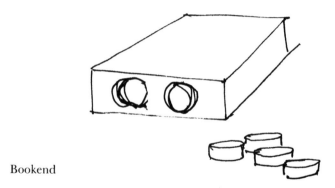

Bookend

Storage of objects other than books

Material such as dust jackets, inserts, and pamphlets requires special storage.

Dust jackets. An original dust jacket in good condition enhances the value of a book. If left on the book dust jackets are subject to fading or abrasion, even with a polyester film dust jacket added on top. They are best stored separately in a box lying on its side, or upright with a piece of acid-free corrugated cardboard scored and folded in the box beside them, or with several sheets of corrugated cardboard cut to size which can be removed as the box is filled. This is so that they won't sag. If the dust jacket is left on the book, it should be removed while reading as the edges are easily frayed, but the polyester dust jacket should be put back on.

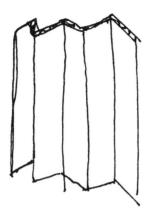

Accordion box filler

Newspaper clippings or other related material. This material can be photocopied on acid-free paper or kept in an acid-free envelope in the book, or, preferably, stored in an envelope or folder elsewhere. A large amount of material should not be stored in a book, as this can deform it and actually break the binding.

Pamphlets. Pamphlets and other limp-cover materials need support and protection. They should be stored in hard-cover pamphlet folders in acid-free wrappers, which can be inserted in envelopes within the outer cover.

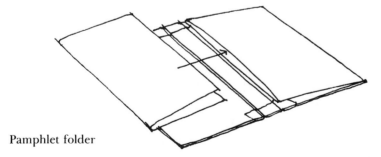

Pamphlet folder

Discrete materials stored in a box. Do not rummage through them to find what you want. They are probably fragile so take them out or put them back in the box with care, being particularly careful if the box is very full. A small amount of material should be stored in the way described for dust jackets to avoid sagging.

Objects. Unusual objects seem to gravitate to book collections. The Yale Library, for instance, has a rose Liszt kissed (and one that Byron kissed, too), some tea leaves (not actual tea leaves but ones that made a beverage similar to tea) sent to James Boswell, and Fanny Burney's thimble. All present interesting storage problems that must be solved as they come along. No blanket guidelines are possible.

Other factors to be taken into account in storing books are prevention of biological attack and theft, and preparedness for flood or fire.

Biological attack

The enemies of books included under this heading are: babies, cats, dogs, rodents, birds, mold, and insects—the last two being the most insidious and difficult to control.

Damage from babies, cats, and dogs is minimal in rare book libraries and slight in private collections. However, all these creatures should be kept away from books.

In 1244, Richard de Bury, in his *Philobiblon*, wrote "Nor let a crying child admire the pictures in the capital letters, lest he soil the parchment with wet fingers: for a child instantly touches whatever he sees." A child can also easily tear a page. Then there is the terrible example of the nursemaid who cut out all the illuminated capital letters in a twelfth-century Bible to amuse her charges. This is probably not a serious danger today.

Although cats usually sharpen their claws on logs, rugs, or upholstery, they occasionally do so on anything else striking their fancy—including books.

Dogs, particularly puppies, chew on almost anything; what is left of a chewed book is usually unusable.

The presence of rodents—mainly rats, mice or squirrels—is indicated by droppings and the mess they leave, such as empty acorn shells on shelves behind books. They eat paper, vellum, leather, glue, paste, and so on. They usually eat inward from the edges of pages and leave very small jagged tooth marks around the eaten area. In addition to eating paper, rodents urinate on it, staining and weakening it.

Mousetraps seem to be the most humane way of dealing with mice. There are Hav-a-hart mousetraps and also ultrasonic devices which emit a beep said to be inaudible to people or pets, but so annoying to mice that they leave.

Call in professional exterminators to deal with rats.

Be sure squirrels cannot get in a building, and do not make pets of them.

Pigeons and other birds can choose to nest in air shafts or attics. In addition to making a mess, they carry a variety of damaging insects and should be discouraged or at least kept out with screens over air shafts or other openings to the inside.

Domestic insects—so called because they live with man —include termites, cockroaches, bookworms, silverfish, firebrats, book lice, and book mites. They are ubiquitous in both temperate and tropical climates, and most of them prefer warmth and darkness.

An excellent book on domestic insects is *Urban Entomology* by Walter Ebeling (University of California, Division of Agricultural Sciences, 1975). It identifies the insects and gives methods of getting rid of them.

Books are taken from shelves to give to readers, to dust, or to consult, fairly frequently. Any irregularities on the shelves such as dead insects or small piles of cream colored dust (the excreta of bookworms) should be investigated at once.

Biological attack monitors. No monitors are needed for babies, cats, dogs, or cockroaches. Their presence is manifest.

A simple trap for bookworms (the larvae of a variety of flying beetles) and silverfish or firebrats can be made. This indicates their presence but does not get rid of an infestation.

Glass evaporating dishes, 3″ in diameter, should be coated on the outside with flour paste to enable insects to climb up the slippery sides. Put a teaspoon of wheat flour in each dish and place them on low bookshelves, several to a room. The flour attracts adult beetles and the take-off area is too small for them to fly out of the trap.

Bookworm trap

In a large library, a map of the position of the traps is helpful. They should be checked at regular intervals.

Extermination of insects

A wide variety of insecticides, more or less toxic, is available. Spray-type insecticides should not be used on books.

Termites. They are not a serious threat as they will presumably be dealt with long before they start on books. They can be heard eating inside a piece of furniture or wall and will, of course, be exterminated as soon as detected. Exterminators are usually listed under Pest Control Services in the Yellow Pages.

Cockroaches. They eat paste and glue and will eat through bindings to get to it. They also excrete a dark, staining liquid.

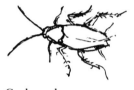

Cockroach

Do not allow food or drink near books, as these attract cockroaches.

It has been said that cockroaches spend their leisure time grooming themselves. They therefore ingest anything they walk on. Boric acid powder spread behind books (care must be taken not to put it where domestic animals might walk in it) will get rid of cockroaches.

Where there are no domestic animals it can be put under and around the base of shelves also. A very simple applicator is a dowel rod, cut in about 2″ from one end with a slightly porous sock or cloth filled with boric acid power tied to it. Tap it lightly along the shelving. This deposits a light coating which is all that is needed. It usually takes several weeks for an application of boric acid to take effect.

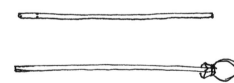

Boric acid applicator

Bookworms. As already mentioned, bookworms are the larvae of a great variety of beetles. They feed on digestible materials in the paper, making lace of it, and sticking pages together. They also feed on the leather and glue of the bindings, and wooden boards, if any. In addition, they eat through sewing thread so that the books fall apart. The adults can fly long distances.

Adult beetle (enlarged)

Outward evidence of infestation is the presence of dead adult beetles on the shelves (those in the Beinecke Library were about ⅛″ long and dark brown). There will also be piles of light granules under or in front of the books on the shelves. These granules (the excreta of the larvae) will also fall out of the book if it is tilted back on the shelf. The adults bore their way out of books in order to mate so there will be small round holes on the spine, particularly noticeable on vellum books.

Inside the books there will be live larvae in holes. They are not shy and will rise in their holes if touched with a pencil point.

Bookworms can be exterminated by freezing the infested books. Neighboring books should be frozen as well. See "Freezing to kill insects." The area where there has been an infestation should be checked frequently.

Silverfish and firebrats. These pests will also indicate their presence by getting caught in bookworm traps. They usually come out at night and will eat through covers to get at the starch and gelatin beneath them. Silverfish prefer cool, damp areas, and firebrats, warm ones. They are similar in appearance and move very fast. Silverfish are flat and gray; firebrats, a mottled gray.

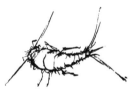

Silverfish

Boric acid powder spread around as suggested for cockroaches will eliminate both silverfish and firebrats. They multiply rapidly so be sure to catch an infestation in its early stages.

Book lice and book mites. These small pests are gray, white, or translucent, and about the size of a pinhead. They are found in large numbers in damp, dark areas and in books. They usually appear in the fall and do more damage (not very visible) than might be supposed from their size. They eat glue, starch, and fungi.

Book lice and mites can be exterminated by freezing, but the best remedy is to provide a dryer climate.

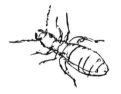

Book louse (greatly enlarged)

Moths. Surprisingly, ordinary outdoor moths can get into a building through a ⅛″ hole. Although they do no damage to books themselves, beetles use the bodies of dead moths as hosts for laying their eggs, so they should be kept out if possible.

Clothes moths will lay eggs in books and under dust jackets, especially in areas of high humidity. The eggs can stain the book and leave paper-like protective casings. Lower the humidity and spray an insecticide in the neighborhood of the books but not on them. Freezing will kill both eggs and larvae.

Freezing to kill insects

Professional exterminators and U.S. Department of Agriculture local agricultural experimental stations are apt to recommend highly toxic methods of extermination. The non-toxic method of extermination developed by Charles Remington, Professor of Biology at Yale, and Curator of Entomology at the Peabody Museum in New Haven, is greatly preferable. This is freezing, which is not harmful to books or toxic for people.

Although freezing at 6°F in a domestic freezer will kill beetles and all other book-eating insects at *all* stages—eggs, larvae, pupae—or adult—blast freezing at −20°F for 72 hours has been used at Yale. This is probably overkill.

If books are very damp, they should be allowed to dry out for a week or so before being frozen. This prevents the formation of ice crystals.

The books to be frozen should be sealed or well wrapped in plastic (preferably polyethylene) bags and should be left in the bags until the condensation on the outside has evaporated after the books have been taken out of the freezer.

Mark books that have been frozen if the books are to stay in the wrappers for any length of time so that they will not be frozen again by mistake.

The larvae turn black when frozen and should be left in the books until they dry out (several days) to keep them from smudging the paper when they are removed.

For details of the Yale program see "The Yale Non-toxic Method of Eradicating Book-eating Insects by Deep-freezing," by Kenneth Nesheim in *Restaurator* 6:1984, pp. 147–164. Information on the equipment (commercial freezer, meat trucks, etc.) used in Yale's program of freezing books is available from the Conservation Division of the Preservation Department of the Yale Library. Ask for "Insect Extermination by Freezing."

Any books from areas that are suspect—barns, the Near East, etc.—should be frozen before entering the collection.

Mold and fungus

Mold grows at a temperature of 70°F and a relative humidity of 65% in stagnant air. Its growth can be prevented and/or controlled by maintaining a stable relative humidity no higher than 60%, and preferably around 50%, a temperature below 70°F, and good air circulation.

Fungus growth such as foxing (brown spots on paper, the cause of which is not clearly understood) is also controlled to a large extent by proper storage conditions.

Human Error and Mutilation

Thoughtful housing and handling can wipe out human error and careful surveillance is the best antidote to mutilation.

FLOOD

The National Preservation Program Office at the Library of Congress and the Northeastern Document Conservation Center can give advice on disaster recovery, and the American Institute for Conservation of Historic and Artistic Works (AIC) will give you the names of fellows in your area, some of whom may have had disaster-recovery experience.

Leaking water pipes, malfunctioning air-conditioning units, inadvertent sprinkler system use, and excessive rain can all cause minor flooding.

Water can cause damage out of all proportion to its amount. As already stated, mold forms at a temperature of 70°F and 65% RH in stagnant air. In the case of wet books, *mold can form within 48 hours or less*. It is therefore very important to take every precaution against the possibility of flooding and to be prepared to act quickly if a flood does occur. The general objectives are:

1. To stop the influx of water and get rid of the water in the area.
2. To assure the safety of personnel entering a flooded area with standing water.
3. To identify and remove the wet material from the flooded area in an orderly manner.
4. To freeze or dry the material within 48 hours or less by freeze or vacuum drying, or by hand.
5. To assess the damage and notify your insurance company.
6. To dry out and disinfect the flooded area if necessary.

It is sometimes difficult to get an insurance appraisal right away. It may be a good idea to point out to the insurance people that, as wet books sit and mold forms, the cost of restoration increases hourly.

The location of master light switches, electrical outlets, and floor drains (if any) should be recorded on a floor plan.

Also identify all possible sources of water:

- Steam pipes
- Bathrooms
- Sinks
- Cooling equipment
- Radiators
- Windows and skylights

In addition, there are always unexplainable leaks. If possible, store books away from all possible sources of water.

If there is any history of leakage from the outside, cover bookshelves with a plastic drop cloth and place pans so as to catch the water if a major storm is predicted.

A water alarm for as little as ⅛″ of standing water is useful for alerting one to water on the floor but is obviously no use for monitoring water dripping from a pipe.

For disaster recovery, have the following materials available, the amounts depending on the size of your library:

- Medium-heavy plastic drop cloths to cover shelves if water is coming in from above
- Sponges

- Clean rags
- Paper towels
- Freezer wrap
- Plastic milk crates (to carry and store wet books)
- Pails

Freezing wet books buys time. List the telephone number of a freezing facility, usually listed under "Warehouses, cold storage" in the Yellow Pages, with your other emergency numbers. It is advisable to talk to an officer of the company before any flooding occurs, to find out if they are willing to take in wet books on short notice. It is also advisable to list the home phone numbers of one or two officers of the company as floods inevitably occur on weekends when only a caretaker is on duty at the warehouse.

Removing books to a dry area. Plastic milk crates, which hold about a cubic foot of material, are a good size for moving wet books, which can be very heavy.

Drying by hand, fan drying. Stand the books, fanned out, on their heads on several layers of paper towelling or unprinted newsprint. Let one or two fans play on them. This is for books that are not saturated. If possible support the text block to the height of the squares with a truncated pie-shaped piece of styrofoam. This is really a counsel of perfection and not practicable if a large number of books is involved.

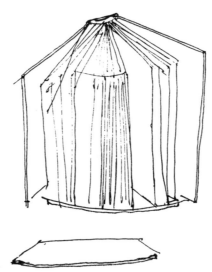

Styrofoam support

Drying softcover books. These must be dried by interleaving or hanging up on a clothesline if they are not too heavy.

Drying by hand, interleaving. This must be done with extreme care as wet paper tears very easily.

Paper towels or unprinted newsprint can be used to interleave at intervals of about 25 leaves (50 pages). The interleaving should be changed frequently, so this method is very time consuming.

When books are almost dry (still slightly cool to the cheek) they should be closed and the drying finished under light weights.

Coated paper. This paper usually sticks together if it has been wet and then dried. The leaves of some coated papers can be successfully separated under water, but the entire surface of others will slide off if fully immersed. Vacuum drying is said to dry coated paper without causing the pages to stick together.

Preparing books for freezing. Books should be tightly packed in plastic milk crates. Cloth covered books will not stick together so need not be wrapped. Books with coated paper or plastic covers will stick to adjacent books so should be wrapped in freezer paper.

Freeze or vacuum drying. In vacuum drying water goes straight from ice to vapor. Coated paper will not fuse into a block and swelling and consequent distortion of the book is minimal. This process seems to be preferable, but one does not always have the choice as both types of facility are at a premium. Books should be frozen before they are sent to a drying facility.

A home freezer can be used, but rapid freezing is best. Since there are very few freeze-drying facilities for books, they must sometimes be held in storage, at −15 to 20°F, until the facility can take them.

Wei T'O has developed a freeze dry/exterminator. Write them for the address of the local institutions that have these units (see Appendix).

There are now firms that dry out whole buildings and claim to dry everything in them. They do this by drawing out wet air while constantly pumping in dry air. If, indeed, this method proves satisfactory and safe for objects and books, it should replace present methods of drying. Some monitoring to be sure the books are not dessicated would probably be needed. At present there are very few firms that do this.

Severe water damage in a large library

A great deal has been written on this subject. The following plans, available from the respective institutions, will be helpful in making a plan fitted to your library: *Disaster Prevention and Preparedness* by Hilda Bohem, Berkeley, University of California Task Group, 1978, and "Disaster Response Plan" by Jan Merrill-Oldham, University of Connecticut.

A revised edition of the classic on the subject, *Procedures for Salvage of Water-damaged Library Materials* by Peter Waters, Library of Congress, is now available.

There are two cautions: *Do not enter an area flooded with standing water until it has been declared safe to do so by a person from the local electricity company. Do not attempt to clean or repair damaged, wet, or muddied books.* Leave this to conservation or preservation personnel.

Steps to be taken before a major flood:
Prepare a directory of business and home telephone numbers for:
• Members of the administration to be notified (librarian, business manager, head of conservation/preservation, etc.)
• People willing to help in salvage
• Freezer warehouse
• Local freeze-dry facility
• National Preservation Program Office, Library of Congress; Northeastern Document Conservation Center.
Both have had experience with the aftermath of floods.
Have the following materials and equipment available:
• Portable electric water pumps and a 1¼" flexible hose
• Gasoline-powered water pump
• Water vacuums
• Floor squeegees (if there are floor drains)
• Freezer paper dispenser, mounted on a book truck
• Freezer paper

- High-velocity oscillating fans
- Portable dehumidifiers
- Heavy-duty extension cords
- Grounded plug and screw-type adaptors
- Plastic milk crates
- Small flat-bed trucks
- Flashlights
- Plastic drop cloths
- Large and medium plastic bags
- Large self-stick labels
- Scissors
- Pails and sponges

If a flood occurs, take the following steps in this order:
1. Notify the appropriate people.
2. Appoint the person to be in charge of salvage operations.
3. Secure the flooded area with signs, barriers, or guards when it has been declared safe to enter.
4. Create maximum air flow by opening doors and windows, and start fans if possible.
5. Appoint a person to man an emergency phone. Inform all the people involved in salvage of the name and number.
6. Estimate the cubic footage of wet material so arrangements for freezing can be made.
7. Call up sufficient support personnel.
8. Get rid of the water with pumps or water vacuums. Two people are needed to empty a vacuum with 15 gallons of water as it weighs 100 pounds.
9. Pack the material in milk crates and label them.
10. Freeze the wet material.
11. Arrange for an appropriate drying method.
12. Mop up any residual water in the flooded area —particularly under shelving.
13. Bring in dehumidifiers. Monitor the RH if possible.

Rare book libraries are often called by distraught victims of floods. It is a good idea to have a summary of helpful information for them. This should be available to all the staff likely to answer the telephone. It could read as follows:

INFORMATION FOR FLOOD VICTIMS

Names and telephone numbers of:

Local disaster recovery firms, if any
Local freezer warehouses
National Preservation Program Office (202) 707–1840
Northeastern Document Conservation Center
   (508) 470–1010
AIC (202) 364–1036

Caution against entering an area with standing water.

Recommend drying or freezing as soon as possible as mold can form within 48 hours or less at 70°F and 65% RH.

Recommend maximum possible air circulation.

FIRE

The obvious causes of fire are incendiarism, defective electrical equipment, careless smoking and exposure of paper-based materials to overheating—beside steam pipes, for example.

Detailed information on fires in libraries—prevention, detection, and extinguishing them—is contained in the National Fire Protection Association pamphlets, NFPA 910, *Protection of Libraries and Library Collections*, 1985, and NFPA 74, *Household Fire Warning Equipment*, 1984. If you send for one (or both) of these pamphlets you will also receive the NFPA catalog, which lists their staggering number of pamphlets on every aspect of fires.

Several Yellow Pages in the telephone book are devoted to Fire under headings such as Fire Alarm Systems, Fire Extinguishers, Fire Protection Equipment, and Sprinklers —Automatic—Fire.

It is a good idea to get in touch with your local fire department so that they will know the layout of your library and the problems they might encounter in fighting a fire in it. In the Beinecke Library, which is a very complex building, there is a centrally located map to show firemen how to get from here to there. The doors in the building are marked with color-coded symbols, and, just in case some fireman is color blind, the symbols are also coded by shape.

Fire prevention. According to the NFPA, "A high standard of housekeeping is the most important single factor in the prevention of fire." Other factors are:

Safe containers for wastepaper or any combustible materials, particularly concentrations of paper products.

Regular inspection and maintenance of electrical, heating, air conditioning and fire protection equipment. Heat attracts dust and causes dessication. Both are fire hazards, so all electrical equipment should be kept free of dust. Dried out wires or parts of motors should be replaced.

Smoking should be forbidden.

Fire detection. There are three types of fire detection systems: smoke, heat and flame. All are designed to give early warning.

The detectors can be either "spot" (small and round) or "line" type (lengths of heat-sensitive wire or small-bore metal tubing). Heat detectors cannot detect small smoldering fires. See Fire Alarm Systems in the yellow pages.

Fire extinguishing systems. If at all possible, smother a small fire with a heavy cover such as a rug.

The chemicals of fire extinguishers are damaging to books, but if books are actually alight it differs very little whether they are burned or damaged by chemicals. Hand fire extinguishers, preferably using Halon 1301, should, of course, be available and their position marked on a floor plan.

Any extinguishers containing bicarbonate of soda should be avoided as any residue can change the pH of materials which in turn can change their color.

Halon gas extinguishes fires by inhibiting the chemical reactions of fuel and oxygen. It may not extinguish deep-seated fires, but will extinguish surface ones. It is not thought to be damaging to books except in that its rapid release from nozzles (it is stored in cylinders under pressure) may dislodge objects in its path. Halon 1211 total flooding system is prohibited in normally occupied areas but Halon 1301 can be used there with safeguards.

Carbon dioxide, dry chemical, or high expansion foam systems are damaging, if not fatal, to people. (According to the NFPA manual, on the subject of carbon dioxide systems, "Personnel must evacuate before agent discharge to avoid suffocation.") No information is available on what they do to books.

On-off automatic sprinkler systems. Although, as already stated, water is extremely damaging to books, a little water is better than a lot, such as that from a fireman's hose. An automatic on-off sprinkler system minimizes the amount of water damage by turning off when the temperature returns to normal. Safeguards against inadvertant turning on of these systems should be provided.

The value of automatic on-off systems is that they detect a fire at its point of origin, cause the sounding of alarms, and control or extinguish the fire before it has time to spread.

Protection of Libraries and Library Collections lists a number of library fires in which the damage in libraries with sprinklers and automatic fire detection equipment was in the thousands of dollars, while that in libraries without this protection was in the hundreds of thousands if not millions.

Fire deterrents for individual books. Don Etherington, formerly Conservator at the Harry Ransom Humanities Research Center (*Abbey Newsletter*, October, 1986, p. 72) made the following observations after a serious fire where there was considerable damage from heat as well as from the fire itself:

Books that had been oiled resisted the heat better than those that had not been treated. The drier the book, the greater the damage.

Leather bindings and labels, including those in glass-fronted cases, were frizzled or looked bubbled. This was particularly so on the upper shelves where the heat was most intense. The reason for this has not yet been determined although it may have been due to the rapid decrease in humidity. Wherever possible, store leather bindings on the lower shelves.

Books in glass-fronted cases were better protected than others.

Polyester dust jackets (pages 116–119) preserved books noticeably. Those with jackets retained their gilding and shape better than those without.

Cleaning books after a fire. In cleaning up after the fire it was found that the following methods were most successful in removing smoke and soot:

Pink Pearl erasers worked better than anything else.

Damp sponges worked best on smooth cloth, but did not work well on paper.

Extra fine steel wool left the surface of leather bindings intact beneath the soot.

Chemical sponges left residual film and smell behind and the books resisted further cleaning.

These methods have not been fully tested but are certainly promising, except for the last one.

Removing the smell after a fire. Thorough airing on a clear, slightly breezy day helps remove the smell left by a fire. Stand the books, fanned out, on a table in the shade. Do not leave them overnight.

Fire Damage Restoration firms which claim to remove smells are listed in the yellow pages.

THEFT

Overall security measures are, of course, a necessity. They range from locks on doors to elaborate electronic systems which usually monitor fire as well as theft.

Monitors. Many yellow pages in most city telephone directories are devoted to Burglar Alarm Systems, most of which list twenty-four-hour, central-station monitoring. A reputable dealer can design a security system to fit your needs.

Closed circuit television surveillance systems. These are advisable in rare book reading rooms, where their value is largely that of a deterrent. Readers should not be seated with their backs to library staff or monitors.

Other protective measures. Have readers leave briefcases or purses at the desk.

Limit the amount of material to be given to a reader at one time.

Even though books are safest when carried in boxes, take them out of boxes before giving them to a reader. Having the books themselves visible facilitates checking their return.

Check, and count if appropriate, all items when they are

given to the reader and when they are returned at the end of the day.

If you provide pads for note taking, have a hole bored in the center of each. A dowel rod can be put through the hole and the pad can then be shaken to release any papers concealed in it. Separate sheets of paper may be more appropriate.

Most of the following information has been taken from the admirable booklet, *Rare books and manuscript thefts, A security system for librarians, booksellers, and collectors* by John H. Jenkins, available from the Antiquarian Booksellers Association of America, 50 Rockefeller Plaza, New York, NY 10021.

Reporting theft. If the value of the stolen material is over $5,000, or the individual items are worth more than $100 each, telephone the FBI (listed in the United States Government section in the telephone book). Next notify your attorney and your insurance agency. Do not publicize the theft in the media immediately after it takes place as this may result in the destruction of the books.

Report missing items to the A.B.A.A. National Headquarters (address above) and to BAM-BAM (Bookline Alert: Missing Books and Manuscripts) a service of *American Book Prices Current*. Information on the missing item/s will be instantaneously available to dealers and libraries in this country and Europe. For more information, write BAM-BAM, c/o *American Book Prices Current*, 121 East 78th Street, New York, NY 10021. The *AB Bookman's Weekly*, Missing Books Section, P.O. Box AB, Clifton, NJ 07015, will publish a list of stolen material for a small fee. It is assumed that the thieves have already sold the books by the time the list appears so that it will alert the new owners, not the thieves.

A list of the stolen material should include: author, title, date, edition, physical description of condition, and any identifying stamps, book plates or markings and their location.

If the theft includes manuscript or autograph material notify the Society of American Archivists, 330 S. Wells St., Suite 810, Chicago, IL 60606.

Proof of ownership. It is sometimes difficult to prove ownership. In addition to ownership marks, page 106, clear photographs of the binding, the title page, or a page with identifiable discolorations, or with bibliographic idiosyncrasies, will be helpful in doing so.

The A.B.A.A. booklet urges prosecution if a thief is caught.

If your books are recovered, notify the organizations that have listed their theft.

Return of stolen books. If you find that a book you have acquired has been stolen from someone else, you are morally and legally bound to return it to the owner and stand the loss of its cost. If the owner is nice, he or she will share the cost (usually half) with you, but this does not always happen.

Buying books that are suspect. You can check on such books by calling BAM-BAM, (212) 737–2715.

3

The Handling of Books

Christopher de Hamel, in *A History of Illuminated Manuscripts*, points out that books have a knack of surviving. He goes on to say that while the first monastery in England, Saint Augustine's in Canterbury, has been a ruin for centuries, over two hundred and fifty of its books still exist today—as do our battered books from childhood rather than the tricycles or airplanes.

Although the following "do nots" may seem like cases of "Go see what Master Alfred is doing and tell him not to," they really can prolong the life of books and help to keep them in good condition.

Do not lean on a book. This can crack the adhesive on the spine.

Do not use a book as a support for writing. Your pen or pencil can make an indentation through the paper you're writing on.

Do not underline or highlight. This is disfiguring and annoying to other readers, time consuming to erase if it is in pencil, and otherwise often impossible to remove.

Do not write in or near a book with a pen. Any kind of ink spot can be irreversible. Use a pencil instead.

Do not rest your hands on illuminations or handwriting. Moisture in them can smear paints or inks and even slight abrasion can cause pigment to flake off. Oils transferred to a book can attract fungus or insects.

Do not mark your place with your finger. This puts a strain on the spine where the book is sewn and the gatherings adhered.

Do not mark your place with eyeglasses or other objects. This can mark the pages as well as put a strain on the spine, particularly if the objects are left in the book for any length of time.

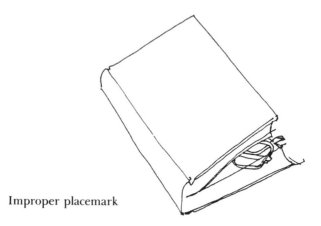

Improper placemark

Do not turn down corners to mark your place.

Do not leave a book open, face down. This can cause cracking of the spine. If a book is left open, right side up, for any length of time the spine can also crack.

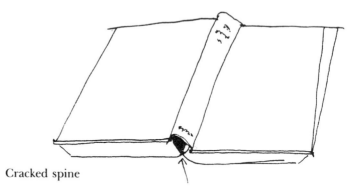

Cracked spine

Do not use rubber bands to hold together a book that is falling apart. Sulphur in the rubber is affected by ozone and will eventually break or become sticky. Use cloth tape, ½" or more wide if possible, or a polyester film strip fastened with Velcro or double-faced tape.

Do not use paperclips, staples or pins in books. They can rust, dig into the paper, and tear it when they are being removed. If paperclips are found in a book, remove them by bending them apart. Bend up the legs of staples with a dull knife or letter opener before removing. Pins can also rust and are sometimes hard to remove. Hold the paper down firmly on either side of the pin and pull it out, parallel to the plane of the paper, with needle-nosed pliers.

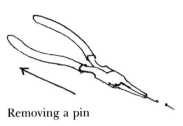

Removing a pin

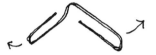 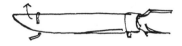

Removing paperclips and staples

Do not press flowers in books. They will stain the pages.

Do not mend paper with pressure-sensitive tape of any kind. It will discolor the paper and is extremely difficult to remove.

Do not try to remove pressure-sensitive tape yourself. It is easy to lift the surface of the paper with it. Tape removal is a job for an expert.

Do not use self-sticking memorandum notes. They leave a slight residue, particularly if left on for any length of time, which will attract dirt in the future. If they become wet, they are very difficult to remove, and fragile leather and other surfaces often adhere to the notes' adhesive. Their paper is acidic and the color may run.

Do not pile more than a few books on top of each other. There is danger of the pile toppling or a book being knocked off. This is a hazard particularly where there is inadequate processing space. Stack books carefully in order of diminishing size.

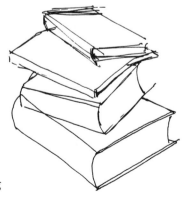

Improper stacking

Do not put a book down where anyone has been eating. There may be a slight reside of grease.

Do not lick your finger or use a pencil eraser to turn a page. Pages can be turned without these aids, with care.

Do not breathe or cough on a page in close examination.

Do not keep liquids on the same level as a book. Always keep them at a lower level.

There is a sign at the door of one rare book library:
No Smoking,
No Eating,
No Drinking
in the building
This is good advice.

There are more "do nots" that will come along in the appropriate places, but there are also a good many positive things that can be done to care for books properly. After climate control comes good housekeeping. Common sense will be your best guide.

General cleaning. Since people, books, curtains and carpets all create or exude dust, frequent vacuuming of the floors is recommended.

Before having floors washed, cover the lower shelves with plastic drop cloths to ensure that no liquid splashes on the books. This may also be done when rugs are cleaned.

Cleaning shelves, dusting only. This can be done one shelf at a time which simplifies keeping the books in order.

Remove all the books on a shelf to a book truck or table. Remove them a few at a time (the number depending on their size). See Taking books off the shelf, pages 98–100.

Vacuum the shelf or dust it with a One Wipe dust cloth. These cloths are specially treated, dustless, lintless cloths that can be washed up to twenty times and still retain their effectiveness.

The books can be cleaned and returned to the shelf immediately.

Cleaning shelves, washing. Usually shelves need only be washed at long intervals. Use a mild detergent.

Several shelves should be washed at one time as they must have enough time to dry thoroughly before the books are replaced.

The books can be cleaned and put on a book truck or on a table in piles of two or three, the containers or piles labeled sequentially as to location on the shelves.

Cleaning books, dusting and vacuuming. Most dust collects on the head (top) edge of books, and is best removed with a vacuum cleaner.

The vacuum cleaner should have cheesecloth placed over the hose opening and under a brush so that, if any piece of the binding (such as a loose label) is detached, it can be retrieved to be replaced later. Any loose pieces should be put in an envelope labelled with the call number or title.

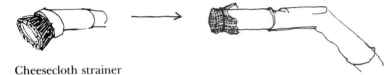

Cheesecloth strainer

Although it is not as strong, and using it would be more time consuming, a Mini-vac can be used instead of a large vacuum cleaner for cleaning the head edge.

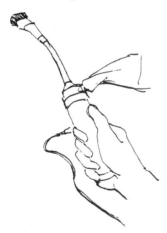

Mini-vac

If air pollution has deposited a greasy coating on the head of a book, it will need to be wiped with a dustcloth. Use a One Wipe dust cloth.

The head edge of a book should be cleaned first. Hold the book as shown in the drawing so that the dust will fall away from it, and dust or vacuum away from the spine. Hold the book tightly closed so that the dust will not work

Position of book for dusting

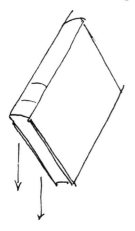

down between the pages. Dust the head and then the rest of the book. Never clap books together to remove dust.

Cleaning leather bindings. Leather bindings can, of course, be cleaned with saddle soap, but *moisture can cause blackening and cracking of some deteriorating leathers.* Do not use saddle soap on gold tooling, and do not wash turn-ins. Judicious leaving alone is probably best here.

However, if it is absolutely necessary to wash a binding, do so as follows:

Rub the surface of the soap with a moistened sponge to form a lather.

Rub the lather into the leather.

Wipe off excess with a clean, damp sponge and dry with a lint free cloth. Let the book dry thoroughly before reshelving it.

Cleaning cloth bindings. There is a substance called Bookleen Gel which does brighten colors, at least temporarily, and is said to clean gilt edges. The smell is somewhat persistent. Although it may have no permanent effect, it probably does no harm. Apply it with a small piece of cloth, using a circular motion. Let it air dry briefly.

Cleaning paper and paper bindings. This must be done with great caution. Use a soft brush, such as a Japanese one or one of those used by artists and architects. Brush out toward the edges, being particularly careful if the paper is torn. Brush lightly.

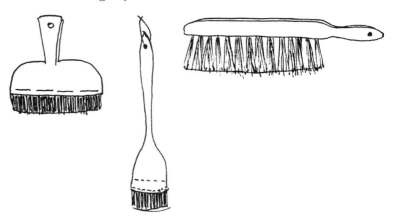

Paper cleaning brushes

Do not use a dust cloth as it may grind the dirt into the paper. Little information is available on the relative damage done by dirt and the various cleaning powders and erasers available. Crumbs of cleaning powders can be left on the paper and even the gentlest eraser can abrade and/or leave a residue. However, so can sharp dust particles.

If an eraser is used to lighten or remove spots, erase the spot itself lightly, and then erase more lightly still, out from the spot so that the erasure is not sharply delineated. A Magic Rub eraser is the gentlest and the Pink Pearl the strongest. Use extreme caution in erasing.

Read *Curatorial Care of Works of Art on Paper: Basic Procedures for Paper Preservation*, 4th rev. ed., by Anne F. Clapp (New York, Nick Lyons Books, 1987), before cleaning paper inside or outside of a book.

Mending tears

Mending with Japanese tissue and rice or corn starch has proven safe over the years and is reversible in water. The pages of a book need enough mending to be able to bend without further damage. Widely overlapping tears can be reinforced at the edge only; all others should be reinforced along their entire length. Corners need not be replaced.

As a general rule, mend only as much as is absolutely necessary.

Supports for mending. Prop the book open so that the torn page lies flat and supported.

When a tear extends beyond the bookblock, a level support must be built up with other books or cardboard.

Put waxed paper under all mends to prevent moisture exchange.

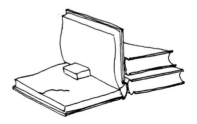

Supports for mending

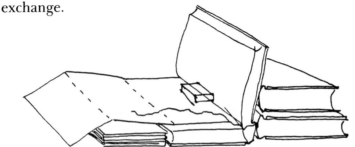

Built-out support

Mending strips. It is important that the grain of mending strips run parallel to their length as otherwise they will wrinkle and lose their strength. The grain direction of Tengujo and Kizukishi runs parallel to the chain lines which are lighter than the rest of the paper and about 1″ apart (see page 108). Hold the sheet up to the light to see them.

Fragile paper may break along the edge of a reinforcement. Torn mending strips are best as they provide a diminishing reinforcement that is much less likely to do so.

Mending strips may be torn by running a wet cotton swab, such as a Q-tip, along a straight edge. Remove the straight edge and pull the strip away from the sheet in the direction of the arrows so that the fibers are splayed out.

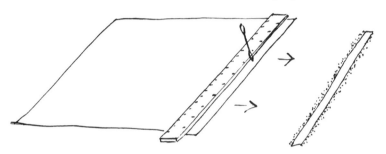

Tearing a mending strip

Pasting. Materials needed are:
Japanese tissue, Tengujo or Kizukishi
Rice starch or cornstarch paste
1″ oil painting brush
#6 watercolor brush
Microspatula

Paste on a waste sheet, being careful that the fibers stay splayed out. Leave one end unpasted so the strip will be easy to pick up.

Put a piece of waxed paper underneath the tear before starting work. Any excess paste could stick the sheet to the bench or a page to the following one. Waxed paper also prevents moisture exchange.

Overlapping tears. Paper often tears in such a way that the edges of the tear overlap. The overlap is usually clearly visible and frequently changes direction. If it does, paste both overlapping edges with a watercolor brush, pasting

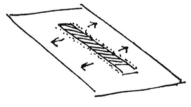

Pasted mending strip

on top of B and under A or the reverse. Be sure the tear is aligned along its entire length before pressing the edges together lightly. You may prefer to paste the overlap in one direction and let it dry before pasting the overlap in the other direction.

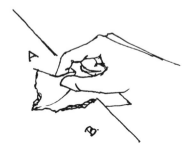

Overlapping tear

Adhere a small reinforcement at the edge of the tear.

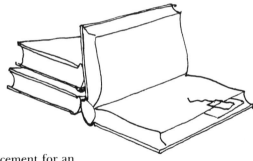

Edge reinforcement for an overlapping tear

Put a piece of waxed paper over the tear, rub down with a bone folder, and close the book. Let the mend dry overnight, under a weight.

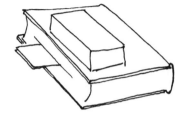

Drying a mend

Trim the mending strip flush with the edge of the page when it is dry.

Reinforced mend. A tear with little or no overlap needs reinforcement. Align the tear and put a small weight on either side of it to hold it in position.

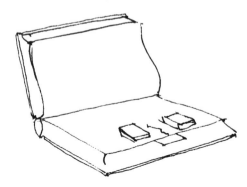

Paste a mending strip slightly longer than the tear. If the tear is a long one, pick up the strip with the pasted side toward you. Put a microspatula against the pasted side of the strip and lift it into a horizontal position, pasted side down.

Position the strip on the tear, leaving the unpasted section overhanging the edge and slide the microspatula out from under the strip.

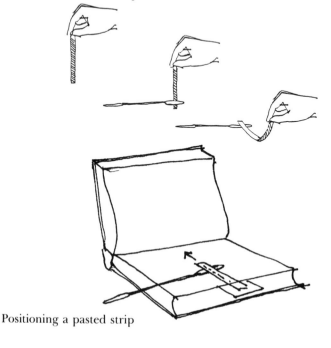

Positioning a pasted strip

Put a piece of waxed paper over the mend, rub down, close the book and let the mend dry overnight, under a weight, and trim, as with an overlapping tear.

Small edge tear. This only needs a small reinforcement pasted and adhered as described above, or no mending at all.

Cleaning gutters

A great deal of dirt can collect in the gutter margins of books over the years, and they should be thoroughly cleaned, particularly if any eraser crumbs remain after cleaning pages. The Mini-Vac or a 1″ oil painting brush are good for this.

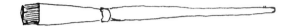

Oil painting brush

Cleaning metal bosses or fittings

These should not be cleaned. It is impossible to do so without getting cleaner on the book itself, and an old book with polished metal attachments looks wrong. All parts of the book should look the same age.

Leather "protector"

A mixture of potassium lactate and p-nitrophenol was at one time recommended to neutralize acids caused by polluted atmosphere and replace the natural salts used in tanning but later washed away. Although still available, it is now thought to be damaging and should not be used.

Leather dressing residue

At one time a French leather dressing called *Cire 212* was often used. A gray residue resembling mold may be found in the indentations of tooling. It can be removed with a small amount of cotton wrapped around the rounded end of a toothpick.

Oiling leather bindings

Over-oiling has caused a great deal of damage over the years. Too much oil can penetrate through the leather and spine linings into the paper of the book, and removing it is a lengthy and expensive process that involves taking the book apart. Over-oiling causes some leathers to become sticky.

Never oil vellum, tawed skin (usually white and frequently pig skin with the holes made by bristles evident), or suede-type leathers. Some paper or synthetic coverings have been made to look very like leather and only if they have been abraded somewhat can you see that their fibers do not resemble leather fibers. They should never be oiled.

Oiling darkens leathers and should never be used on fine "decorator" bindings where colors are an important element in the design, unless the leather is extremely dry.

Oiling does not help books suffering from the form of deterioration known as "red rot." It just makes more of a mess.

However, oiled books suffer less damage from the heat of a fire than unoiled ones, and careful selective oiling is certainly recommended.

When to oil? This is a question that is often asked and is difficult to answer. If books are stored in a very dry environment they will probably need to be oiled every year or so, whereas books stored in a proper environment will need oiling very seldom. Many eighteenth century bindings that have never been oiled and look dry, brighten immensely after oiling. The answer probably is: oil when the bindings look dry. Do not feel you must oil on a regular basis.

How to oil. You will need:
Leather dressing
A small square of soft cloth for putting on the dressing
2 saucers
Paper waste sheets
A soft cloth for polishing
A work table and a table for oiled books
Plastic drop cloths for both tables

The leather dressing recommended is made of 40% anhydrous lanolin and 60% neat's-foot oil, both natural animal oils. It was developed by the New York Public Library and has been tested by the U.S. Department of Agriculture.

Cover the tables with the plastic drop cloths so as not to leave any residue of the very greasy dressing after oiling.

Separate full, half, and quarter bound books. Plan to oil books of approximately the same size at one time.

Put some leather dressing in a saucer and put another saucer nearby for the oiling cloth.

Oiling full leather bindings. Hold the book with the boards held away from the bookblock. Rub a thin coat of oil over the whole outside of the book and the edges of the boards. Do not try to oil the leather turn-ins. It is impossible to avoid getting grease on the pastedowns.

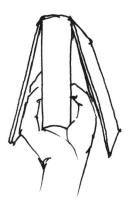

Holding a book for oiling

Some people recommend putting the oil on with the fingers since that makes it easier to control the amount. However, this is very time consuming, and the combination of the circular movement of the fingers and the pressure needed to rub a small amount of oil in must put a strain on the hinges.

When the book is oiled, put it down on a waste sheet on the storage table and put a waste sheet on it before putting another book on top of it. This prevents the books from sticking together. Do not pile more than a few books on top of each other.

Let the dressing soak in overnight and polish the book gently but thoroughly with the soft cloth.

Oiling half and quarter bound books. These books are a nuisance to oil. Oil very carefully, just short of the edge of the leather. You can mask off the paper or cloth side with a strip of paper if you wish. Put two sheets of waste paper on top of a book before adding another.

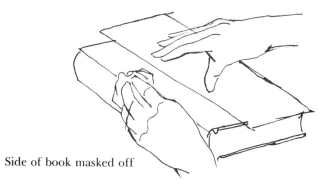

Side of book masked off

Oiling very heavy books. Put the book on a table and oil the side and half the spine. Turn the book over using both hands, put it down on a waste sheet, and oil the other side and half the spine.

Consolidating leather. Klucel G (hydroxypropylcellulose) is a non-ionic adhesive which dries clear and is very flexible. Mix a 2% solution with ethyl or isopropyl (rubbing) alcohol.

    1½ tsp. (3.7 gr.) Klucel G
    1 cup (185 ml.) isopropyl alcohol

Let the mixture sit overnight or longer, stirring occasionally or shaking the container as Klucel G is slow to blend. A peanut butter jar with a wide mouth is a good container as it can be closed and a wide brush will fit into it.

Klucel G does a wonderful job of consolidating leather. The solution sinks in and evaporates in a very few minutes, so one side of the book can be painted, the book can be put down on a piece of waste paper, and the other side painted. Klucel G darkens the leather very slightly. It can be used on suede-type leathers without flattening the nap but it can cause sheepskin to delaminate more than it does naturally. It is not a panacea so use it with discretion. The solution lasts indefinitely and need not be refrigerated.

Apply the solution with a 2″ brush. Klucel G is water soluble so the brush may be washed out (thoroughly) in water.

Photocopying

As already mentioned, pressing a book down on a flat surface can crack the spine. However, an electroluminescent photographic process (see list of suppliers, pages 141 and 150), which allows copying from books so tightly bound or fragile that they can scarcely be opened, has been developed by the British Library and is available. Another solution is to forbid all photocopying of tightly bound books. A single signature pamphlet, sewn through the fold, will not be harmed by photocopying, so the prohibition could be selective.

Photocopy on archival paper.

Photocopying does have the advantage of cutting down on the use of original material. However, most readers do not like to work with photocopied material.

Opening a new book

Hold the bookblock at a right angle to a flat surface with the boards spread out. Let a few pages on either side fall down and run you hands gently along the gutter. Repeat this process until you reach the center and the book lies flat (if well bound).

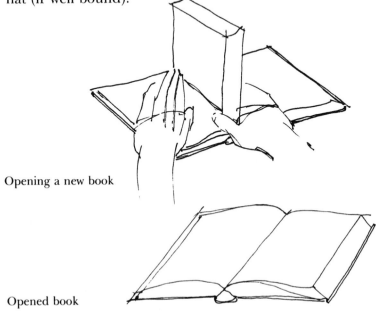

Opening a new book

Opened book

Opening edges

There is a distinction between cutting and opening. The edges of a book are cut in the process of binding; they are opened, if necessary, when the book is to be read. Even though you believe that a book is more valuable with unopened edges you may wish to read it.

A folio does not need opening as it has no folds at head or fore edge; a quarto has folds at the head only; an octavo has folds at the head and fore-edge.

To open edges cut with a dull knife held parallel to the plane of the paper. Cut out, away from the book.

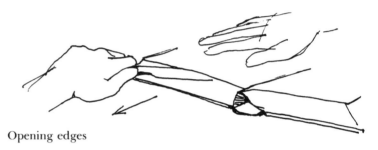

Opening edges

Handling

Most damage occurs to books when they are transported or studied—that is to say, handled. Handle books gently. Never force them to do anything.

For a start, clean hands are a necessity. "Please be sure your hands are clean and dry" could be included in a handout on handling. See Reader education, page 107. Some people advocate wearing white gloves to look at fine books. This seems excessive, and clumsy, as gloved fingers could tear pages.

Handling supports. Books require support at all times —when being read as well as on the shelf. The boards of a

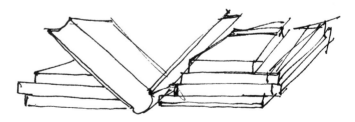

book shouldn't be bent back beyond the plane of the open book as this can damage the joint. The board can be supported with another book or with foam rubber wedges, perhaps with a felt cover over them. Lecterns, which can be tilted at various angles, cut down on actual handling. Books can be held open with bean bags. The bean bags can be long, filled with shot, and made of velvet, which does not slip on the pages and looks very elegant. Position the bean bag on the outer margin of the page.

Small books can, of course, be well supported and held open by the human hand.

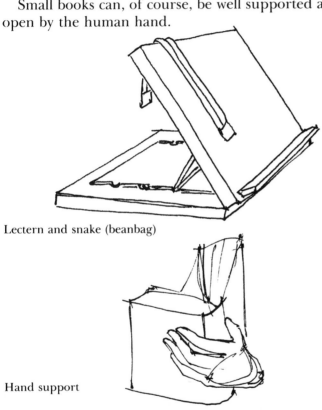

Lectern and snake (beanbag)

Hand support

Shelving books. When books are first moved into an area they should be shelved rather loosely until they have had time to adjust to the environment—say for two or three weeks. When they have adjusted they should be shelved, neither too loosely nor too tightly, and upright, supporting each other. Loosely shelved books are apt to become what dealers call "shaken," that is, loose in their covers or deformed, and tightly shelved books are hard to take off the shelf. Attempting to force a book onto a shelf can cause another book to pop out.

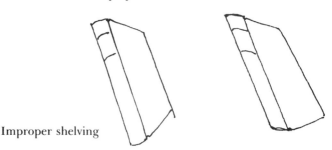

Improper shelving

Do not shove books sideways on a shelf, as this puts a strain on the joints and abrades the tail edges of the boards.

Very large books should be stored on their sides, one to a shelf if possible, or no more than three or four, depending on their thickness and weight.

Soft cover books should be stored flat unless some form of rigid support is provided. See page 63.

A large book shelved beside a small one eventually splays out. The exposed area also fades even if not exposed to strong light. Books should therefore be grouped by size on the shelves. Octavos, up to 28 cm (ca. 11″); quartos up to 40 cm. (ca. 15¾″); and folios over 40 cm (ca. 15¾″) are standard groupings.

Miniature or small books, under 10 cm (4″), should either be shelved separately or boxed in comparatively tall, filled-in boxes. See page 120.

Taking books off the shelf. People often take books off the shelf by pulling on the headcap or pinching the joints with their fingernails. These methods can break the headcap at head or tail or tear cloth and paper hinges.

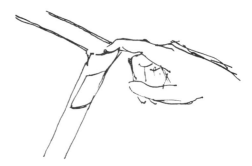

Wrong

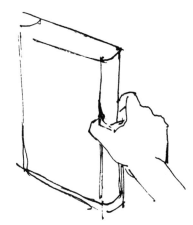

Wrong

A book can be tilted slightly forward, or the adjacent books pushed back, and the book can then be taken from the shelf by gripping it firmly at the middle of the spine. Take the time to adjust a book end when you have taken a book off the shelf.

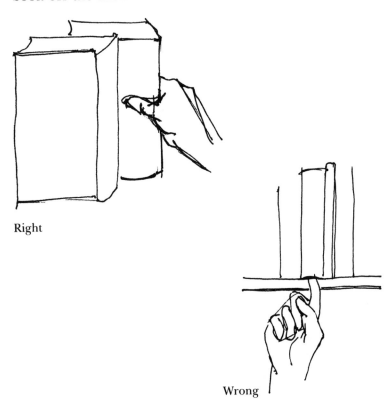

Right

Wrong

Do not try to take a book off a shelf that is too high to reach easily. Use a kickstool or library ladder.

Picking up a book. Pick up a book so that there is no strain on the hinges and joints. Never pick up a book by one board as this does put a great strain on hinges and joints.

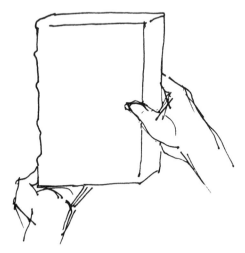

Supporting a heavy book

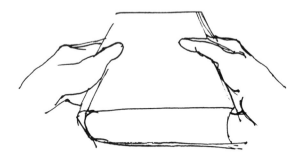

Use two hands to support a heavy book.

Very large, heavy books are best removed from the shelf by two people, one at the head and one at the tail.

Taking several books off the shelf at one time. Take only as many as you can hold safely with one hand (this depends on their weight) and hold adjacent books upright until they can be held with a bookend or other books placed on their sides.

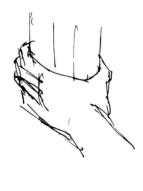

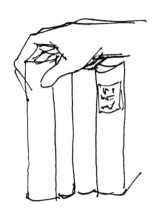

Taking several books off a shelf

Turning pages. Catch the edge of the page with your finger and bend it gently and slightly forward, holding it in an area blank on both sides. Blowing on the edge of pages that are hard to turn is said to help. As already mentioned, do not lick your finger or use an eraser to turn pages.

Use two hands to turn very large pages such as those of newspapers or Audubon elephant folios. They tear easily if turned with one hand.

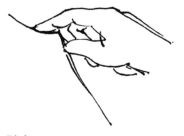

Right way to turn a page

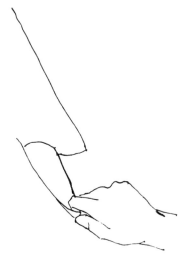

Wrong way to turn a large page

Do not riffle through a book when in a hurry to find the page you want. This can tear the edge of a page.

Bending brittle paper can cause it to break along the bend. Keep brittle pages as flat as possible, opening the book at a right angle only.

Moving books

Books should, as far as is possible, be kept in sequential order when being moved—whether by hand or on a cart.

Do not try to move too many books at one time if you are moving them by hand (as opposed to using a book truck). Carry only as many as you can hold securely. Remember that you may need to use one hand to open a door unless you are lucky enough to have automatic doors or a companion.

Loading a book truck. In loading a truck the books should be placed standing upright and securely supported. Do not place them on their fore-edges or spines. Spines could be abraded and putting them on fore-edges causes them to pull away from the binding, particularly if they are left on the truck for any length of time. Folios should be laid flat, and books should never be placed on the heads of other books. Be careful not to overload the truck. A bicycle inner tube may be used to stretch around the truck and prevent catastrophes.

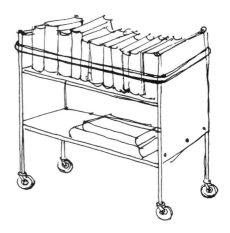

Properly loaded book truck

Packing books in crates or cartons. Pack them, spine down, fairly tightly, in medium sized cartons or milk crates which are about 1' square. They need not be wrapped in paper unless their binding is fragile or their surface can rub off. The cartons or crates should be enclosed in plastic bags if there is any possibility of rain during a move from one building to another. Number the containers to facilitate reshelving in order.

Bookplates

As you may have gathered from reading this book, all the materials in contact with books should be acid free—including bookplates. These can be printed, engraved, typographical, calligraphic, or illustrative and should be small, as a large bookplate will warp the board of a small book if fully pasted. They should be printed on acid-free paper, preferably with the grain of the paper running parallel to the spine of the book.

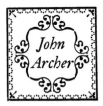

Good size for a bookplate

Leather bookplates are acidic and discolor the adjacent paper and should be avoided, as should gummed or pressure-sensitive bookplates.

Stark white bookplates look awful in early books.

Fragile book bookplates. These are frequently needed. The following one is used in one library:

> *This book is extremely fragile. Please handle it with care so that it will be here when you want to refer to it again.*

Fragile book bookplate

Do not rebind bookplate. A boxed book in a condition that shows an interesting structure could have the following bookplate adhered in the box:

In its present state this
book provides valuable
information on binding structure.

Please do not have it rebound
or restored.

Bookplating. If there are the bookplates of previous owners inside the front board, your bookplate can be put inside the back one.

If the inside of a board is interesting in any way—a decorated pastedown, ownership marks or an interesting board attachment in an early book—tip the bookplate in along one edge or at a corner only.

For very small books, simply write your name lightly with a No. 2 pencil. As already mentioned, writing your name (permanently) in a book is thought by some to decrease the resale value, although on the other hand provenance is considered very important, and a name and date written unobtrusively in a suitable spot (not on the title page) can scarcely be considered detrimental. Your name and the date are part of the history of the book which is important. For some reason bookplates do not seem to affect the value of the book. Perhaps it is because they can usually be removed.

All three of the following pastes are water soluble and suitable for pasting bookplates:

Wheat paste:
¼ cup (59 ml) water
3¼ tsp. (6 gr.) dry wheat paste

Put the water in a container and add the wheat paste gradually, stirring constantly until the paste is smooth. Let it sit for several hours before using. Store covered without refrigeration.

Cornstarch paste:
½ cup (118 ml) water
2 to 2½ tsp. (6–7 gr.) cornstarch

Dissolve the cornstarch in the water and cook over medium heat, stirring constantly until the paste is translucent. This takes about one to three minutes. The paste can be stored, covered, without refrigeration and will last several days. Stir if it separates.

Rice starch paste:
⅔ cup plus 5 tsp. (200 ml) water
5 tsp. (10 gr.) rice starch

Put in the top of a double boiler and cook until it is translucent plus about 10 minutes. Store, covered, at room temperature.

Paste molds quickly. One or two drops of formaldehyde on a cotton ball taped to the top of the paste container helps prevent the formation of mold.

Bookplates are apt to curl when pasted and this makes them difficult to handle. They can be flattened before they are pasted by wetting them with a damp sponge or running water on them and then blotting them with a paper towel. They will soon relax, uncurl, and be easy to paste. Paste with a pastry brush or cheap house-painting brush, on a waste sheet and throw the sheet away before you proceed.

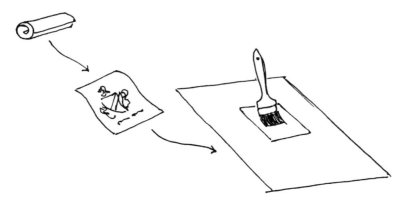

Flattening and pasting a bookplate

Build up a support of boards (wooden and/or binders board) or books, under the cover, position the bookplate, put a clean waste sheet on it and rub it down with a bone folder.

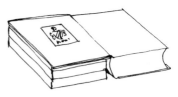

Supporting the board

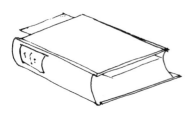

Extending moisture barrier

Put a piece of polyester film or waxed paper under and over the bookplate to prevent moisture exchange when you close the book. Let it extend slightly so you won't forget to take it out. Let the bookplate dry overnight.

Bookplating several books. Paste an area of marble, lithographer's stone, or formica large enough for several bookplates (three or four for a start). Relax them, put them down on the paste, and cover them with waxed paper to prevent their drying out and sticking. Smooth the waxed paper down so that the bookpaste is thoroughly pasted. Peel the waxed paper back, exposing one bookplate at a time, and adhere it in the book.

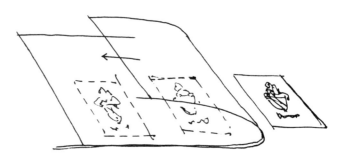

Bookplating several books

Other ownership marks

Embossed or perforated ownership marks are irreversible and deface the book. They should not be used.

Secret ownership marks are probably a good idea in today's world and are a test for your ingenuity. They should be no more than a dot and their position should vary in accordance with some system you have worked out. There should perhaps be a register of such marks, or how could you prove that a mark was yours, but this would perhaps defeat their purpose. See also Proof of ownership, pages 79–80, and "Guidelines for marking rare books, manuscripts, and other special collections" in *Rare books and manuscript thefts*.

Acid barriers and other materials

Book boards are often acidic. An acid barrier of good paper or polyester film can be put inside the cover, loose, to prevent acid migration. The barrier should be about $1/16''$ larger than the pages in both directions.

Bookmarks and paper for notations. These should be acid-free as they are sometimes left in books. Scrap paper provided for readers should also be acid-free for this reason.

Any notes left in a book by previous owners or readers should be removed. If there is pertinent information on them, the page or folio number where they were found should be written on them in pencil and they should be stored elsewhere, suitably identified.

Flags. Flags for call numbers, cut from thin Bristol board or very stiff paper, should be acid-free, with their grain long. An average size is $8\frac{1}{2}'' \times 1''$.

Charge slips. These should not be left in books but often are, so they too should be acid-free.

Reader education

This is not a problem in a private library, as presumably an owner and friend look at a book together. However, it is a problem in a rare-book library.

A handout, or handouts, elegantly designed and printed, which helps insure that they will be read, could be given to the reader when he or she is waiting for a book to be brought out. It could say:

Please be sure your hands are clean and dry.

Please handle fragile books *very* gently.

Please use our acid-free bookmarks to mark your place. Acidic paper left in a book by mistake can discolor the paper it touches and cause it to deteriorate.

Please take notes in pencil. Pencil can be erased, ink cannot.

Notify a librarian of damaged or missing pages.

Never force a book to do anything.

Give a book all the support you can.

PROTECTIVE CONTAINERS FOR BOOKS

The urge to wrap a precious object seems to be universal and dates back to very early times. There are examples from Egypt, England, Germany, Ethiopia, Tibet, and doubtless many other places. Protective containers, all helpful, can range from dust jackets to beautiful, gold-tooled leather boxes lined with velvet. Knowledge of a few easy techniques is needed to make simple protective containers.

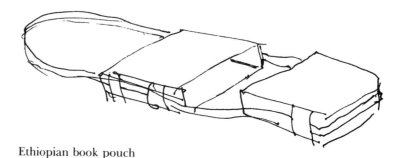

Ethiopian book pouch

Grain. The alignment of the fibers in paper is called the grain. Paper products bend most easily parallel to the grain direction. To determine grain direction, bend paper or Bristol board, first in one direction, then in the other and press down gently on the fold. You will feel less resistance in one direction than in the other. The direction of least resistance is the direction of the grain.

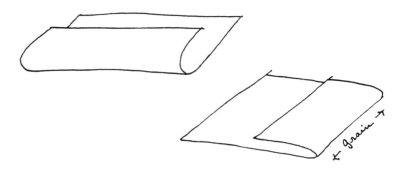

Determining grain

Scoring and folding. The line where a bone folder scores is not exactly at the edge along which you are scoring, but half its own thickness away from that edge.

To score exactly on a mark, put the point of the bone folder on it and bring the edge against which you are scoring up beside the bone folder.

Score firmly, two or three times, depending on the thickness of the board you are using. Keep the scoring edge in place, holding it down firmly, and bend the board up at a slight angle with the bone folder.

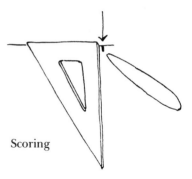

Scoring

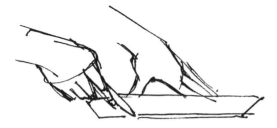

Bending

When all the folds in a board have been scored and bent slightly, bend each one all the way over and rub down the fold with a bone folder (bone folders are stronger than your fingers). The folds will follow the lines of the initial bending.

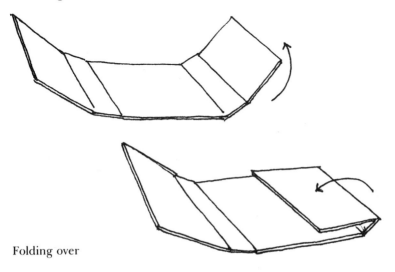

Folding over

Cutting. If possible, use a cutter or board shears for cutting. If this is not possible, cut with a utility knife or scalpel along a metal straight edge.

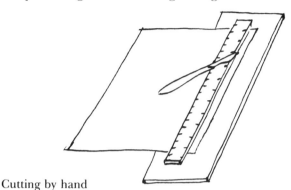

Cutting by hand

Cut on a piece of waste cardboard or the "self-healing" surface available in art-supply stores. This prolongs the life of the cutting blade. Change the blade as soon as it becomes dull.

Put the straight edge down along the edge to be cut and press down firmly on it. Cut once or twice as it is easier to cut with several light cuts than with one heavy one.

To cut a rectangular piece of material, make two marks equidistant from an edge. Make a parallel cut, lining up a straight edge with the marks.

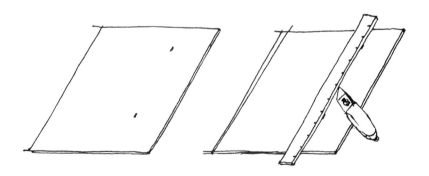

Making a parallel cut

Cut the other two sides at a right angle to your parallel ones.

Protective wrapper

The idea for a simple, easy to make protective wrapper for small or medium sized books originated under Willman Spawn at the American Philosophical Society in Philadelphia, and this version was developed by Hedi Kyle, now the Conservator there. It is described here with her permission. These wrappers keep books virtually free of dust and protect them from abrasion. They are easy to make so they can easily be replaced if necessary. Protective wrappers for new, pristine books should be made as soon as they enter the collection.

The advantage of home-made protective containers over standard sized, ready-made ones, even though the latter may be made of heavier materials, is that they can easily be made to fit exactly, while the books may rattle around in standard sized ones.

The equipment and materials needed are minimal.

Equipment.
> Metal straight edge
> Utility knife or scalpel
> Triangle, a large 40°–60° one
> Bone folder
> Scissors
> Toothpick
> Adhesive container

Materials.
> Acid-free Bristol board, .010 available in sheets 20″ × 30″ or 48″ × 72″ or .020 (preferable) available in sheets 40″ × 60″
> PVA (Polyvinyl Acetate Emulsion) such as Elvace or Sobo

Measurements.

Height: Put a waste strip of paper on the book and mark the height.

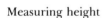

Measuring height

Width: The rounding of the spine must be included in this measurement. Put a triangle against the spine of the book and measure from it to the fore-edge.

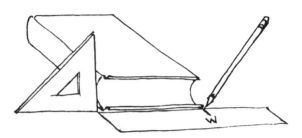

Measuring width

Thickness: Measure this with a combination square and transfer the measurement to the paper strip.

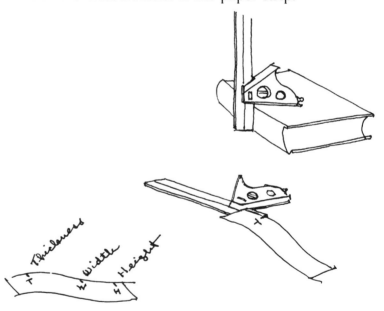

Measuring thickness

Inner wrapper. Cut a rectangle, (page 110), of .010 or .020 Bristol board the height of the book by 2½ times the width, plus 3 times the thickness less ¹⁄₃₂″ at one end. The drawing will make this clear.

Cut off these corners. This can be done by eye, with scissors.

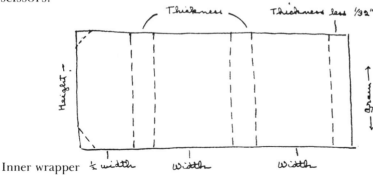

Inner wrapper

Score with a triangle or mark the dimensions on the opposite edge and score and bend as described on page 109. Marking both edges is usually a more accurate method than using the triangle.

Outer wrapper. Cut another Bristol board rectangle the width of the book by twice the height plus $1/32''$ plus twice the thickness. Score and fold this rectangle.

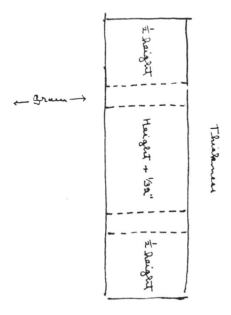

Outer wrapper

Cut a triangle, large enough to accommodate your thumb out of the right edge.

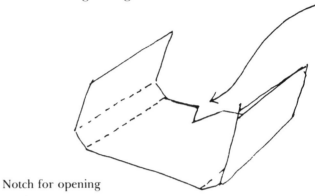

Notch for opening

With a toothpick put three or more dots of PVA (Polyvinyl acetate emulsion, a strong adhesive such as Sobo) about ¾″ in from the left edge of the outer wrapper.

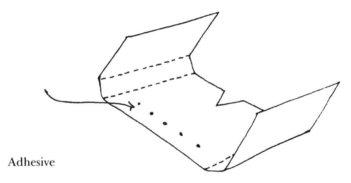

Adhesive

Position the inner wrapper on the outer one.

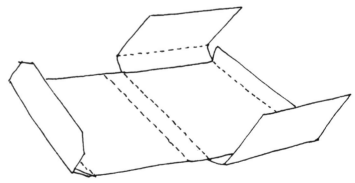

Finished wrapper

Close flaps A and B and bring flap C around and in between the inner and outer wrappers underneath the book.

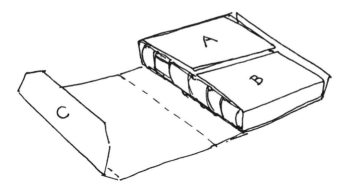

Finished wrapper with book

Asterisks or other symbols can be used on a typed label both for decoration and for cutting guides.

The wrapper is held shut without additional fastening.

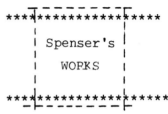

Typewritten label

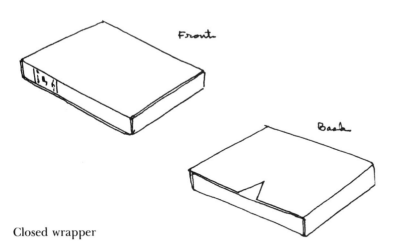

Closed wrapper

Protective dust jackets

As already mentioned, polyester film dust jackets help protect books from the intense heat of a fire. They also protect them from dirt and abrasion.

Commercially available dust jackets have acid-free paper linings which means labeling the book unless you use call number flags. A special pen is needed to write on polyester film. Obviously, labeling is not needed for transparent jackets.

Polyester film is available in rolls 20″ or 40″ wide by 100′ long. The 20″ roll is easiest to handle, but can be wasteful.

Making a dust jacket. Mark four times the width of the book, less 1″ plus the width of the spine at each edge of the roll of polyester film.

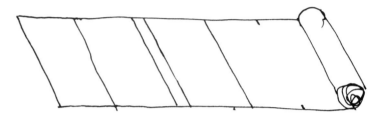

Marking the width of a dust jacket

Line up a straight edge with the marks and cut on a piece of cardboard or a self-healing surface.

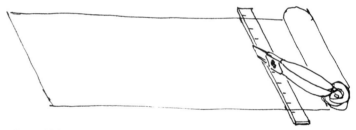

Cutting width

Mark the height of the book at each end of the jacket and cut in the same way.

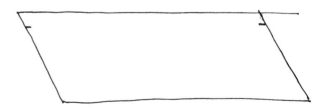

Marking height

Pinching or a short cut with scissors are easy ways to mark polyester film.

The spine folds can be made as follows:

Fold end A over end B leaving the width of the spine (judged by eye) exposed. Be sure the top and bottom edges are lined up.

Rub down the fold with the edge of a bone folder. This gives a sharper crease than using the flat of it.

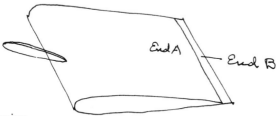

Creasing spine

Turn the jacket over and repeat this process, with end B over end A. In making a jacket for a thin book be careful not to rub down on top of the first crease as this can flatten it somewhat.

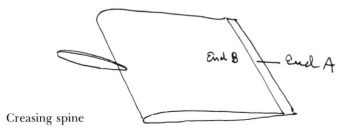

Creasing spine

This produces folds at the edge of the spine in the center of the jacket.

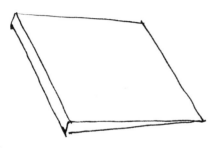

Spine creased

Wrap the jacket snugly around the book.

Fold the upper flap in along the edge of the board and crease along it.

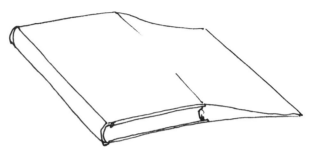

Fore edge folds

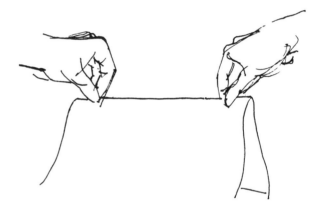

Fore edge folds

Fold the jacket back and crease again, this time with the bone folder.

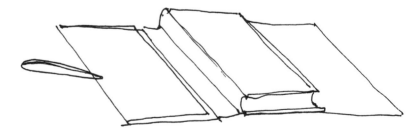

Creasing fore edge fold

Repeat this on the other side.

Having the flaps extend nearly to the hinges has two advantages. The jacket stays on better and the polyester film acts as an acid barrier if the boards are acidic—which they often are.

To anchor the dust jacket more securely, a strip of polyester film may be wrapped around each board and secured with double-faced tape.

Boxes. The books that need boxes are:

Books of great value

Fragile books

Books with protrusions that might damage adjacent books

Vellum books

Miniature books

Books in important bindings

Unbound manuscripts

Commercially available boxes. Such boxes, of archival quality, are now to be had in a bewildering array of sizes and shapes. Some of the firms that provide them are listed in the section on Materials and Suppliers.

Custom made boxes. These call for the services of a book binder. Write the Guild of Book Workers, 521 Fifth Avenue, New York, NY 10175, for the names of book binders in your area. The Guild cannot evaluate their members' work, so you will have to do that yourself. A nearby rare-book library may be willing to tell you the names of the hand binders who do work for them or the commercial library binder who will make boxes to fit individual books.

Boxes can be of any degree of elegance you care to pay for.

Boxes for parchment manuscripts. These should have clasps to keep the parchment flat.

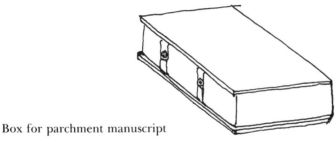

Box for parchment manuscript

Boxes for very small books. They should be of a size comparable to the other books on the shelf, and filled in to the size of the book.

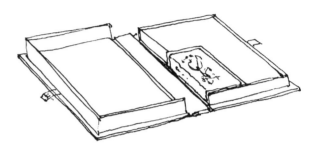

Box for a very small book

Boxes for very heavy books. These can be made with spaces for the hands to grasp the book on both sides.

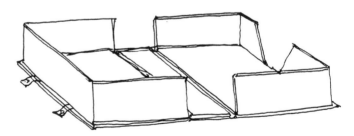

Box for a heavy book

Slipcases. They can abrade a book as it is taken in or out and are to be avoided unless the book is wrapped in a four-way chemise, an awkward and expensive item.

Wraparounds. These are protective covers that are somewhat stronger than the Kyle wrapper. Making wraparounds requires some special equipment, so it is not described here. Detailed instructions are given in my book, *Books, Their Care and Repair*. Wraparounds, custom made and in many standard sizes, are available commercially.

CONSERVATION

It is quite natural for a collector to want his or her books to be as handsome as possible, inside and out. For this reason, until very recent times, collectors have had their books rebound in the best manner of the day—particularly if the original binding was plain, dirty, and shabby, as early bindings often were.

An early example of this is the Victor Codex at Fulda. Victor of Capua finished reading the book on April 12, 547, but the present binding, which is said to have belonged to Saint Boniface, was probably bound in the first half of the eighth century.

Although the practice of rebinding has produced many interesting, idiosyncratic bindings, particularly for private collectors, there is a certain monotony in a whole national library bound in one color with the king's arms on the side —even if it was done in the seventeenth or eighteenth century. Needless to say, such wholesale rebinding is an enormous loss to the binding historian.

Collectors today want their books to be as close to the original state as possible, and educated taste calls for careful cleaning if needed, the minimum of restoration consistent with the safe use of the book, and a protective container.

Cosmetic treatment is acceptable only if a book is seriously defaced.

Treatment options

Ideal conservation treatments should be reversible—that is, able to be undone without further damage to the book. This is unfortunately not always possible.
The options are:
  Paper treatment
  Complete rebinding
  Rebinding without pulling (taking the book apart)

Rebacking
Minor repair
Encapsulation
Protective container provided

Paper treatment. Washing and deacidifying involves pulling, and a decision to do this should be taken only after careful consideration and only if the paper is highly acidic. Pulling often damages the folds of the gatherings, which must then be repaired. This is called guarding. Resizing can be done at this time if necessary.

Tears can, of course, be mended (pages 87–91) by the collector or librarian without taking the book apart, but mending by an expert is preferable.

Complete rebinding

This should only be done if the present binding (probably a nineteenth-century rebinding) is so tight that illumination or text is hidden in the gutter margin, or if the sewing is broken and the cover damaged beyond use as a protection.

Complete rebinding may or may not require the paper treatment described above. The book must be resewn and can then be rebound in a manner suggesting the period of issue. Cloth is a stronger binding material than most present-day leathers.

"Non-adhesive binding" using no adhesive at all in contact with the bookblock is the best kind of binding and should be used whenever possible.

Many parts of the old binding can often be incorporated into a new one. The previous binding, even if it is not contemporary with the book, should be stored with it as it is part of the book's history. Fragments (thread, cords, parts of the cover) can be put in a polyester film envelope also stored with the book.

Other treatments.

Rebacking. This can be done if the boards are detached, or nearly so, and interesting enough to be preserved. The boards are reattached, the spine material removed (lifted), and new material put on the spine and under the old cover for a short distance on the sides. The original spine material can sometimes, but not always, be saved and replaced. Corners also usually need repair. Many rebackings are rebackings of rebackings which used the very poor quality leather in use at the turn of the century. They are particularly troublesome to reback yet again.

Minor repairs. They include mending small page tears, light resizing of edges, and reattaching loose parts of the binding.

Encapsulation. This destroys the book as an object but is sometimes the only alternative for the preservation of very fragile paper. The leaves are cut apart and each one is encapsulated in a polyester film envelope. These envelopes are then bound back together.

Dealer's marks in books. These cryptic marks (usually on a pastedown) can provide valuable information and should be preserved. Be sure that the binder does so.

Limp covers. They can be repaired and the book boxed. Never have such a book bound in hard covers.

Preparing a book to go to the binder. If the boards are off, or the hinges weak, tie the book together with soft cotton tape, with the bow at the fore-edge, and wrap it securely in paper.

Put any detached parts in envelopes, separating bits of the binding and pieces of pages. If you know where pieces of pages go, put each one in a separate envelope with the page number on it.

Do not make the mistake of cleaning the house before the cleaning lady comes—do not try to improve the condition of the book before it goes to the binder.

Conservation and binding are highly skilled and very time consuming so do not be surprised at the high prices asked. They are probably lower than they should be to compensate adequately for the time spent.

Many binders cannot afford adequate insurance coverage. If this is the case, you may want to insure the book yourself.

Taking a long time to bind is endemic to bookbinders so do not let this surprise you. In *Pagan Papers* Kenneth Grahame complained, "Of a truth, the foes of the book-lover are not few. One of the most insidious, because he cometh in friendly, helpful guise, is the bookbinder. Not in that he bindeth books—for the fair binding is the crown and flower of painful achievement—but because he bindeth not: because the weeks go by and turn to months, and the months to years, and still the binder bindeth not: and the heart grows sick with hope deferred.... Then a secret voice whispereth: 'Arise, be a man and slay him!' .... But when the deed is done, and the floor strewn with fragments of binder—still the books remain unbound. You have made all that horrid mess for nothing."

Relations with the binder/conservator. Do not be intimidated by an exhibition of expertise on the part of a conservator. Although he or she can diagnose the physical ailments of your book, and repair it, your knowledge of the book's position in its historical background, in its relation to the other books in your collection, and its monetary and/or sentimental value carry equal weight. The relationship between the curator or owner and the binder/conservator should be a collaboration.

Up to a point, less is more. When in doubt, box. To repeat, *judicious leaving alone is best for books*, and common sense, sometimes lacking in conservation thinking, is also a very important factor in their care.

Travel, Display and Collecting

Collectors and libraries are often asked to lend their books for exhibition. Before lending a book the owner should be able to specify the conditions under which a book is exhibited. The points to consider are the length of time the book is to be exhibited, climate conditions and lighting, security, and methods of support.

Condition report. It is important, both for the welfare of the book and the relationship between lender and borrower, for the lender to write a detailed condition report, a copy of which should be sent to the borrower with the book and a request that the book be examined on arrival, any changes noted, and the form signed and returned to the lender. The borrower should (obviously) keep a copy of the form to check the condition of the book when it is to be returned.

Travel

Having a courier is, naturally, the best method of transportation. Short of this, Express Mail (maximum insurance allowed $500.00) or the next day UPS air service (maximum insurance $25,000.00, no limit on UPS surface transport) can be used. The book or books should be as fully insured as possible, probably by your insurance company if their value exceeds the limit on the amount of insurance Express Mail or UPS will provide.

Wrapping for shipping. Books to be shipped probably

do not need the humidity controls usually included with works of art. However, books need to be very thoroughly wrapped as follows:

Acid-free tissue paper

Plastic to prevent moisture from penetrating

Two wrappings of bubble plastic or an inner wrapping of corrugate cardboard

Strong, corrugated cardboard outer wrapper.

All the above should be thoroughly sealed. The book or books should not be able to move within the package, so fill in as needed.

Very small and very large books do not travel well. Wrap a small book in a fair sized package, filled in, so that the package will not be lost, and provide extra protection for corners and a heavier outer container for large, heavy books.

Unwrapping. Many dealers wrap in the way just described. In unwrapping, be patient and work slowly, being careful not to cut the book when cutting through sealing material.

Display

Books on exhibition are subject to many kinds of unusual stresses such as changes in climate, light on the pages, stresses on joints. Display mechanisms should be unobtrusive and aesthetically pleasing as well as giving the books the support they need.

Time on exhibition. Books should never be left permanently on exhibition; if this is the case (none of us is perfect) the pages should be turned regularly about once a month. This helps prevent excessive fading of one opening and reduces the probability of the spine's cracking. Preferably, books should have periods of rest in the dark, and should not be on exhibition for more than three months at one time.

Light. Some years ago the British Library refused to allow the lighting of a case in which one of their books (a very important one) was to be displayed. Out of nine cases, one was dark. This dramatically emphasized the importance of the book but seems a little more stringent than necessary, although doubtless it was good for the book. A light level of 50 lux (light at that level must be warm) with the source outside the exhibition case is recommended. Incandescent light fixtures should not be put inside cases as they produce too much heat.

Ultraviolet filtering film can be installed on the glass of the cases, and UV filtering sleeves on fluorescent light fixtures within them.

On-off light switches for exhibition cases are a good idea and it may be helpful to involve viewers in the conservation of objects. Another method of cutting down on exposure to light is to have dark, opaque curtains, with a rod in them, attached on horizontal cases. The viewer can turn them back and then reposition them to cover the case. A notice asking the viewer to do so is probably advisable.

Existing exhibition lighting is apt to be higher than is needed. If there are several fluorescent bulbs in a case, one or more can often be removed, depending on whether or not they are wired in tandem, or masked off with aluminum foil if the bulbs are behind frosted glass or diffused with two layers of fiberglass screening.

The ballast unit of fluorescent lights should be outside exhibition cases. Units generate heat, and have been known to catch on fire.

Window curtains should be closed and lights turned off whenever an exhibition is closed or people are not working in it.

Temperature. Temperature should be as low as possible. As viewers are moving a good part of the time in an exhibition area, and may well have kept their coats on, the temperature can be lower than in regular storage areas —between 65° and 70°F.

Relative humidity. This should be between 50% and 60% in the exhibition room. The RH in exhibition cases will be much more stable than that outside them due to the buffering action of the cases and the exhibits themselves.

Climate monitors. Blue scales for light, hygrothermographs for the exhibition room, and small dial hygrometers or thermo-hygrometers in exhibition cases help to educate the public and also show that you care.

Security. Both exhibition cases and the exhibition area should be armed with electronic alarms. If very rare books are on exhibit, there should be a guard in or near the exhibition area.

Holding books open. This can be done with strips of transparent polyester film. Film is available in rolls ¾" to 2" wide. Narrower strips can be cut from these rolls for very small books.

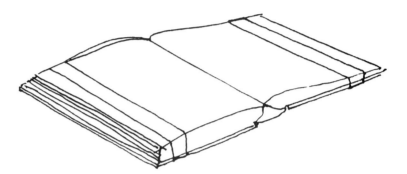

Polyester film strips

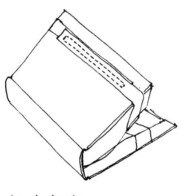

Attached strip

The strips should be more than twice the height of the book. Put a piece of double-faced tape, about 1" to 2", down on one end of the polyester film strip. Fasten the strip snugly around the book, but not so snugly that the pages of the opening on display are distorted.

If the edges of the pages are very fragile, wrap wide pieces of polyester film around them and wrap the taped strip on top of them.

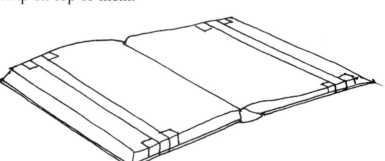

Guards for fragile pages

Plate tissues. Roll plate tissues around a pencil or roll the tissue and clip it with a plastic paper clip on the lower side. Be very careful in doing this as plate tissue is usually very fragile.

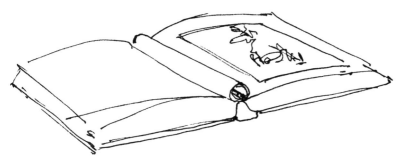

Rolled plate tissue

Supports and cradles. They should be made of neutral colored, yet attractive, materials. Their design varies depending on the way the book is to be displayed—standing up, lying down or slanting, opened near the front, back, or center.

If the book is opened near the front or back, support the board and adjacent leaves so that they are level with the plane of the opening or slightly angled up. Very heavy boards should be almost entirely supported to prevent strain on the joint.

Supports for books displayed this way can be made up of a pile of index or other cards, children's unpainted blocks (painted with acrylic varnish), a pile of small pieces of plate glass (cut to about 1½″ × 4″), letterpress printers' wooden furniture, or any material (preferably neutral) that can be built up to a specific height.

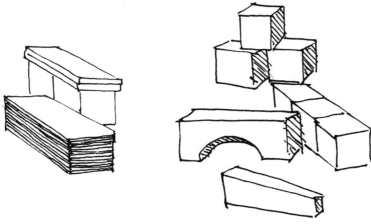

Supports

The supports should be slightly smaller than the board so that they do not show, but most of the cover board should be supported near the fore edge.

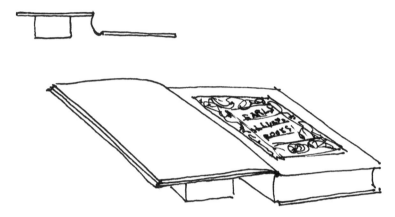

Positioning supports

Wedge-shaped supports and cradles. If the book is to be open in the center, use wedge-shaped supports or a cradle. Making cradles for exhibition is described in detail in *Books, Their Care and Repair*. Wedge-shaped supports can be made of foam rubber or wood, covered with book cloth, or felt, or with a paper or polyester film sheet under the book. At least three-quarters of the height of the book should be supported.

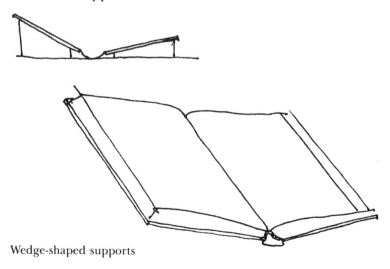

Wedge-shaped supports

Very expensive cradles made of brass and Plexiglas are available. Their advantages are that they are easily adjusted to many angles and can be used over and over.

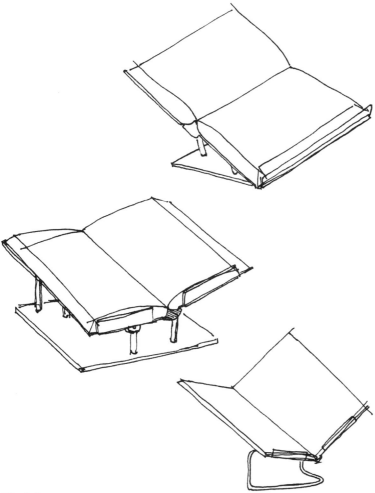

Plexiglas supports

Books displayed upright. Books need to be supported at the tail to the height of their squares (the distance between the bookblock and the edge of the boards) whether they are shown open or closed, as the bookblock of an upright, unsupported book will pull away from the cover. If a book is displayed this way, tape the bookblock together with polyester film and support it as follows:

131

A supply of strips of thin board of various widths and lengths is needed to build up to the correct height. They can be held in place by the polyester film strip holding the bookblock together and look nicer if they are wrapped in a piece of paper or cloth held in place with double-faced tape.

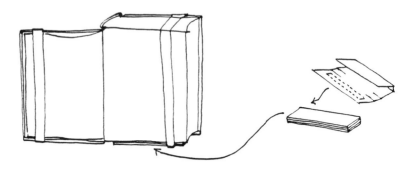

Support for book displayed upright

Do not display books upright unless they are still firmly bound.

If you are displaying both boards of a book at the same time, tape the bookblock together and support it as described above.

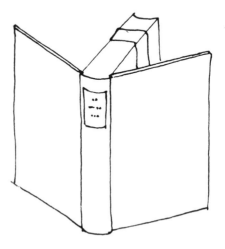

Displaying both boards

Collecting

This book is about the physical care of books that have been already collected, so thoughts on collecting have no valid place in it. However, the following article by Gay Walker is such an excellent summary of the numerous aspects of rarity that it is included here. Some classic books from the large literature on collecting are included in the bibliography.

"The Book as Object" is part of the "Considerations in the Retention of Items in Original Format" and is reproduced from the *RLG Preservation Manual* by permission of the Research Libraries Group, Inc.

THE BOOK AS OBJECT

by R. Gay Walker

This list of considerations has been formulated to aid collection managers and curators in the review of library materials that might be rare and/or valuable. It is an attempt to identify the reasons why books became rare and deserving of retention in their original format.

Many items are important largely or entirely because of their format, and there are often clear reasons to maintain those titles in their original states. In other cases, the reasons may not be so clear, but there may be certain physical elements that should be weighed carefully before contemplating either withdrawal or a conversion to another format for any reasons, including deterioration, space-saving, superseded editions, or duplication. Such a list may provide an incentive to retain those items having significant information embodied in their physical format that might otherwise be lost.

This list was developed by the Preservation Committee [of the Research Libraries Group] with input from the Collection Management and Development Committee and the Manuscripts and Special Collections Task Force. Other documents on this topic were consulted that aided in the compilation of this list including the National Archives and Records Service, document, "Intrinsic Value in Archival Material" (Staff Information Paper 21), "The Transfer of Materials to Special Collections" of the Archives and Special Collections Task Force, Rare Book and Manuscript Section, College and Research Division of the American Library Association, an article on "The Preservation of Bibliographic Evidence" (unpublished) by Ellen McCrady, New York Public Library's Technical Memorandum No. 40 on "Permanent Retention of Materials in the General Collections in Their Original Format," and the chapter on Selection for Preservation Microfilming in the volume on *Preservation Microfilming* edited by Nancy Gwinn (1986).

This is by no means a prescriptive list, and it is not presented in priority order. It does not represent RLG policy and is offered for informational, educational, and selection aid only.

Considerations in the Retention of Items in Original Format

1. Evidential value
   a) Physical evidence associated with the printing history of the item, such as registration pin marks, cancels, printing techniques, paper, and typographic errors
   b) Evidence of the binding history of the volume such as original sewing stations, binding structure, printed wastepapers used in the spine lining, and cover materials
   c) Significant physical evidence added to the volume such as marginalia, marks of ownership, and relevant ephemera laid or tipped in

2. Aesthetic value
   a) Bindings of unusual interest/technique/artistry
      – Historical/developmental interest of structure/ materials
      – Signed/designer bindings
      – Early publishers bindings
   b) Other book decorations of interest (e.g., gilding, gauffering, decorated endpapers, fore-edge paintings)
   c) Illustrations not easily reproducible or meaningful only in the original
      – Color
      – Original woodcuts/etchings/lithographs, etc.

d) "Artists' books" where the book is designed as an object
e) Original photographs
f) Maps of importance
g) Pencil, ink, or watercolor sketches

3. Importance in the printing history of significant titles
   a) First appearance
   b) Important bibliographic variants
   c) Important/collected fine press printings
   d) Indications of technique important to the printing history
   e) Examples of local imprints

4. Age
   a) Printed before [specific dates] in [specific countries] (e.g., all titles printed before 1850 in the U.S., or all books printed before 1801)
   b) Printed during the incunabula period of any area (the first decades)
   c) Printed during specific later periods, such as war years, in specific countries

5. Scarcity
   a) Rare in RLG/NUC/major European libraries
   b) Less than 100 copies printed

6. Association value of important/famous/locally-collected figures or topics
   a) Notes in the margin, on endpapers, within the text
   b) Bookplates and other marks of ownership of such figures; other evidence of significant provenance
   c) Inscriptions/signatures of importance

7. Value: Assessed or sold at more than [specific cost]

8. Physical format/features of interest
   a) Significant examples of various forms as evidence of technological development
   b) Unique or curious physical features (e.g., water-marks of interest, printing on vellum, wax seals, etc.
   c) Certain ephemeral materials likely to be scarce, such as lettersheets, posters, songsters, and broadsides
   d) Manuscript materials
   e) Miniature books (10 cm or less in height)

f) Books of questionable authenticity where the physical format may aid in verification

g) Representatives of styles/fads/mass printings that may now be rare

9. Exhibit value
   a) Materials important to an historical event, a significant issue, or in illustrating the subject or creator
   b) Censored or banned books

Appraising. Knowing the value of your books is important for several reasons—in case of theft, for insurance purposes, including insurance by the binder, and in deciding whether or not to have a book restored. The cost of restoration is often far greater than the monetary value of the book, so the decision to have work done depends on the value of the book in a collection.

Appraising is very expensive, and with reason. An appraisor must be a bookman, that is must have a wide general knowledge of books, bibliography, and other reference material. He then puts a price on the book based on past prices (the value of the book at the point of passing from one owner to another), condition, and rarity.

Dealers' catalogs and *Book Prices Current* are also sources for information on value.

Record keeping. Record keeping and preparing a shelf list are two of the numerous pleasures of the private collector. Samuel Pepys found satisfaction in his catalog: "So home and to supper and then saw the catalogue of my books, which my brother had wrote out, now perfectly alphabeticall, and so to bed."

In a private collection the following information should be kept in a computer data base or a card file, probably alphabetized by author:

Author
Title
Imprint (date and place of production)
Provenance
Date of acquisition
Price
Any additional bibliographical information you consider pertinent

Shelf mark or call number

Shelf list. A private collection should have a shelf list. This is best started at the same time as the collection if its housing is to be permanent. Although it seems pretentious to provide a shelf list for a few volumes, it is an agreeable pastime if done little by little but something of a chore if done all at once for a large collection.

A very simple shelf list can be made by assigning a letter to each section of your bookshelves, numbering the shelves from top to bottom, and the books from left to right.

The shelf-mark of the shaded book is B.3.11.

The shelf-mark can be written lightly in pencil inside the front board, or a small label can be printed with a pleasing border in which to enter the shelf-mark, and, like Mr. Pepys, you can then arrange your books to your most extraordinary satisfaction.

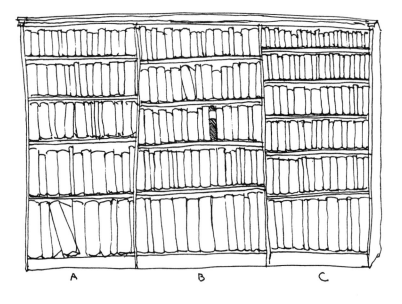

A   B   C

Materials and Suppliers

The materials included in this list are those which are commonly used in the storage or care of books, and are mentioned in this book. The listing of suppliers is, of necessity, partial. You will find that the catalogs of a few of the principal suppliers (easily identified in the following list) are very useful.

In the past, board products usually contained lignin so they are now usually described as lignin-free as well as acid-free. Board is also sometimes described as buffered, or neutral, as some materials, such as photographs, require a neutral container.

Paper can be described as permanent/durable or acid-free. It is usually assumed that it does not contain lignin—except for newsprint, which does.

ACRYLIC SHEETS, PLEXIGLAS, ACRYLITE: Light Impressions, University Products, TALAS*, listed under Plastics in the yellow pages

ADHESIVES: Art supply stores, Conservation Materials, Process Materials, TALAS, Supermarkets, University Products

AIR CLEANERS: see Room air cleaners

ANNUAL AIR QUALITY SUMMARY: Environmental Protection Department, Section on state government in the telephone book

ANTI-STATIC CLEANER: see Plastics in the yellow pages

AQUABOY HUMIDITY INDICATOR: TALAS

*TALAS is an acronym for Technical Library Service, which is why it is in capital letters.

BAM-BAM: *American Book Prices Current*

BINDERS, POCKET STORAGE AND PORTFOLIO: Gaylord

BINDER'S BOARD: Light Impressions (Davey's Acid pHree), TALAS, University Products

BLUE SCALES: TALAS

BOARD, ACID-FREE, LIGNIN-FREE, .040 OR .050: Atlantis Paper, Conservation Resources*, Faulkner Fine Papers, Hollinger, Lawrence & Aitken, TALAS, University Products

BOARD SHEARS: Gane Bros., TALAS

BONE FOLDER: Light Impressions (burnishing bone), TALAS, University Products (Folder, bone)

BOOK TRUCKS: Gaylord, TALAS, University Products

BOOKENDS: Library Bureau, TALAS

BOOKLEEN GEL: TALAS

BOOKMOUNTS: see Cradles

BOOKSHELVES: Library Bureau, Media-Stack, TALAS. See also Library Equipment and supplies in the yellow pages.

BOXES, ACID-FREE, LIGNIN-FREE, BUFFERED: Atlantis Paper, Conservation Materials, Conservation Resources, Coutts Gaylord, Hollinger, Light Impressions, TALAS, University Products

BRISTOL BOARD, ACID-FREE, 32″ × 40″ CREAM AND WHITE: Atlantis Paper, Conservation Resources, Faulkner Fine Papers, Hollinger, Process Materials, TALAS, University Products, paper merchants

BRUSHES: Aiko's, Art supply stores, Conservation Materials, TALAS, University Products, see also Japanese brushes

CARDBOARD, CORRUGATED, ACID-FREE, LIGNIN-FREE: Conservation Resources, Light Impressions, Process Materials, TALAS

COMBINATION SQUARE: Hardware stores

CORN STARCH: Supermarkets

COTTON TAPE: TALAS

*This includes the Conservation Resources branches in England, Canada and Australia.

CRADLES: Benchmark

CUTTER: Gane Brothers, Office supply stores, TALAS

DEMINERALIZING CARTRIDGES FOR HUMIDIFIERS: Brookstone

DOUBLE-FACED TAPE, 3M #415, ¼": Conservation Materials, Conservation Resources, Light Impressions, TALAS, University Products

DOWEL ROD: Hobby shops, lumber yards

DRYING OUT BUILDINGS: Airdex, BMS Catastrophe, SOS International

DUST JACKETS, POLYESTER FILM AND PAPER: Gaylord, University Products

ELECTROLUMINESCENT COPYING: Select Information Systems

ENVELOPES, ACID-FREE: Conservation resources (non-buffered), Coutts Hollinger, TALAS, University Products (non-buffered)

ERASERS, MAGIC RUB, PINK PEARL: Art supply stores

EVAPORATING DISHES: see Laboratory Equipment and Supplies in the yellow pages

EXHIBITION STANDS: Benchmark

FILE FOLDERS, ACID-FREE: Conservation Materials, Conservation Resources, TALAS, University Products

FILMOPLAST P AND P90: Light Impressions, TALAS

FIRE: National Fire Protection Association, Re-Oda Chemical Engineering, Servicemaster

The following headings in the yellow pages deal with fire: Fire Alarm Systems, Fire Damage Restoration, Fire Department

Supplies, Fire Extinguishers, Fire Protection Consultants, Fire Protection Equipment, Sprinklers—Automatic—Fire, see also listings for Flood.

FLAGS: Cut from stiff paper or Bristol board

FLOOD: Airdex, American Freeze Dry, Birchover Instruments, BMS Catastrophe, Cargocaire, Document Reprocessors, Hartford Freezer Co., Munters, National Preservation Program Office, Library of Congress, Loss Control Services, McDonnell Aircraft, Midwest Freeze Dry, Northeastern Document Conservation Center, SOS International, Wei T'O

FORMALDEHYDE: Chemical Supply Houses, Conservation Materials, TALAS

FREEZE DRYING: see firms listed under Flood

FREEZER, COMMERCIAL WAREHOUSES: see yellow pages

FREEZER PAPER DISPENSER: see Paper Distributors (ones that also sell janitorial supplies) in the yellow pages

HAKE BRUSHES: see Japanese brushes

HALON 1301: Brookstone, hardware stores, see Fire Protection Equipment in the yellow pages

HIGH-LOW THERMOMETER: Brookstone, Hardware stores

HUMIDITY INDICATING CARDS AND PAPER: Conservation Materials, Light Impressions, TALAS

HYGROMETER, DIAL: Casella London, Light Impressions, Science Associates, University Products

HYGROTHERMOGRAPHS: Conservation Materials, Light Impressions, Science Associates, University Products

ILLUMINANCE LEVEL METER: Megatron, Science Associates

INDIA INK: Art supply stores

JAPANESE BRUSHES: Aiko's, Conservation Materials, Light Impressions, TALAS, University Products

JAPANESE PAPERS: Aiko's, Atlantis Paper, Faulkner Fine Papers, Light Impressions, TALAS, University Products

KICKSTOOLS: Library equipment and supply firms, University Products

KIZUKISHI: see Japanese papers

KLUCEL G: Hercules Inc., TALAS

LIBRARY STEPS AND LADDERS: Library equipment and supply firms, TALAS

LEATHER DRESSING: Conservation Materials, TALAS

LECTERNS: see Church Supplies in the yellow pages

LIBRARY EQUIPMENT AND SUPPLIES: Library Bureau, Media-Stack, yellow pages

LIGHT CONTROL: Madico, New England Sun Control

LIGHT DAMAGE CALCULATOR: Canadian Conservation Institute

LIGHT METER: see Illuminance level meter

LITHOGRAPHER'S STONE: Rembrant Graphic Arts, TALAS

MAGIC RUB ERASERS: Art supply stores

MELINEX: see Polyester film

METAL STRAIGHT EDGE: Art supply stores, TALAS (heavy duty)

MICROSPATULA: TALAS

MINI-VAC: Computer supply stores, TALAS, University Products

MYLAR FILM: see Polyester film

MYLAR RIBBON: Light Impressions, TALAS, University Products

NEWSPRINT PAPER, UNPRINTED: Art supply stores (in pads), Paper merchants (in quantity)

OIL PAINTING BRUSH: Art supply stores
ONE WIPE DUSTCLOTHS: Supermarkets, TALAS

PAMPHLET FOLDER, HARD COVER: Gaylord
PAPER, ACID-FREE: Conservation Materials, Conservation Resources, Falkiner Fine Papers, Laurence & Aitken Process Materials, TALAS, University Products.
PINK PEARL ERASER: Art supply stores
PLASTIC MILK CRATES: Discount stores
PLEXIGLAS UF3: Light Impressions, Rohm & Haas distributors, TALAS, University Products, see Plastics in the yellow pages
POLYESTER FILM, MYLAR D (DUPONT) OR MELINEX 516 (ICI): Conservation Materials, Pilcher Hamilton, Process Materials, TALAS, Teitelbaum, Transilwrap, University Products
POLYESTER FILM DUST JACKETS: see Dust jackets
POLYESTER FILM STRIPS: see Mylar ribbon
POLYETHYLENE BAGS: Light Impressions
PSYCHRON: Science Associates
PVA (POLYVINYL ACETATE EMULSION SUCH AS ELVACE OR SOBO): Art Supply stores, Conservation Materials, Process Materials, TALAS, University Products

RH INDICATING CARDS: Light Impressions, TALAS
RH MONITORS: Conservation Materials, Light Impressions, Science Associates, TALAS University Products, Vaisala
RICE STARCH: Conservation Materials, Light Impressions, TALAS, University Products
ROOM AIR CLEANERS: Air Cleaning and Purifying Equipment, Air Conditioning Equipment and Supplies in the yellow pages

SADDLE SOAP: Shoe stores, TALAS
SCALPEL AND BLADES: TALAS
SELF HEALING MAT: Art supply stores
SHOT: see Sporting Goods—Retail, or Guns in the yellow pages

SILICA GEL: Conservation Materials, TALAS, University Products

SPRINKLER, AUTOMATIC ON-OFF: see Sprinkles —Automatic—Fire in the yellow pages.

SQUEGEE: see Janitor's Supplies in the yellow pages

STORAGE SYSTEMS, CUSTOM-MADE: Delta Designs

TANK CLEANERS FOR HUMIDIFIERS: Brookstone

TEMPERATURE MONITORS: Brookstone, discount houses, hardware stores, Conservation Materials, Conservation Resources, TALAS, University Products

TENGUJO: see Japanese papers

THEFT: *AB Bookman's weekly,* Antiquarian Booksellers Association, BAM-BAM, FBI

THERMO-HYGROMETERS: Conservation Materials, Conservation Resources (digital), Science Associates, TALAS

THERMOMETER/HYGROMETER: Discount stores, TALAS

TISSUE PAPER, ACID-FREE: TALAS

TRIANGLE, 40–60: Art supply stores

UV ABSORBENT ACRYLIC SHEETS, PLEXIGLAS UF-3 ACRYLITE OP–2: Light Impressions, TALAS, University Products, Plastics in the yellow pages

UV FILTERING FILM: Bonwyke Chamberlain Solar Control, Madico, Solar X, TALAS University Products

UV FILTERING SLEEVES FOR FLUORESCENT LIGHTS: Bonwyke, Conservation Resources, TALAS, University Products

UV MONITOR, TYPE 766: Littlemore, Science Associates

VELCRO: Fabric stores, Conservation Materials, University Products ("Velcoins")

WASTE SHEETS: see Newsprint

WATER ALERTS: Brookstone, Direct Safety, Dorlen Products

WATER TREATMENT LIQUID FOR HUMIDIFIERS:
Brookstone

WHEAT STARCH: Conservation Materials, Light
Impressions TALAS, University Products

WRAPAROUNDS: (protective containers) Conservation Resources

BIBLIOGRAPHY

Care of books.

Baynes-Cope, A. D. *Caring for Books and Documents*. London: British Museum Publications, 1981. An excellent, brief book on this subject by the former head of the Research Library in the British Museum.

Blades, William. *The Enemies of Books*. London: Trubner & Co., 1880. Although not always accurate, Mr. Blades had the root of the matter in him and the book is very entertaining.

Bohem, Hilda. *Disaster Prevention and Preparedness*. Berkeley, CA: University of California Task Group, 1978. Sound, practical advice.

Clapp, Anne F. *Curatorial Care of Works of Art on Paper: Basic Procedures for Paper Preservation*, 4th rev. ed., New York: Nick Lyons Books, 1987. A technical treatment of this subject, clearly presented.

Cunha, George D. M., and Dorothy G. Cunha. *Conservation of Library Materials*, 2nd ed., 2 v. Metuchen, NJ: Scarecrow Press, 1971–72. A useful compendium with an extensive bibliography.

———. *Library and archives conservation, 1980's and beyond*, 2 v. Metuchen, NJ: Scarecrow Press, 1983. The second volume is a supplement to the bibliography in *Conservation of Library Materials*.

de Bury, Richard, *Philobiblon*, Translation by E. C. Thomas, Michael Maclagen, ed., Oxford: Published for the Shakespeare Head Press by Bazil Blackwell, 1970. A book on collecting and the care of books written in the thirteenth century.

Ebeling, Walter. *Urban Entomology*. University of California, Division Agricultural Sciences, 1975. Describes the habits of domestic insects and suggests how to exterminate them.

Greenfield, Jane. *Books, Their care and repair*. New York: H. W. Wilson Co., 1983. Describes simple repairs for 'everyday' books, protective covers, and display cradles.

Horton, Carolyn. *Cleaning and preserving Bindings and Related Materials*. Chicago: Library Technology Program, American Library Association, 1967. One or two things have changed since this book was written, but it is still a very useful work, by one of the most important conservators in this country (now retired).

Jenkins, John H. *Rare books and manuscript thefts, A security system for librarians, booksellers and collectors*. New York: Antiquarian Booksellers Association of America, 1982. Although the listing of specific people to call will, in due course, limit it's value, this is a very useful book.

Kyle, Hedi. *Library Materials Preservation Manual*. Bronxville, NY: Nicholas T. Smith, 1983. This describes simple repairs and also the

'Kyle wrapper' described on pages 111–115.

Library of Congress Preservation Leaflets

No. 1 Preservation of Library Materials: First Sources

No. 2 Paper and Its Preservation: Environmental Controls

No. 3 Being revised

No. 4 Discontinued

No. 5 Newsprint and Its Preservation

No. 6 Audiovisual Resources for Preserving Library and Archival Materials

These are available, free of charge, from the National Preservation Program Office.

Merill-Oldham, Jan. "Disaster Response Plan," Preservation Department, University of Connecticut, n.d. This is very detailed, and could be adapted to other institutions.

RLG Preservation Manual, 2nd rev. ed., Stanford, CA: The Research Libraries Group, Inc., 1986. This is a very thorough manual and the information is sound, if perhaps more than one wants to know.

Rempel, Sigfried. *The Care of Photographs*. New York: Nick Lyons Books, 1987.

Sandwith, Hermione and Sheila Stanton. *The National Trust Manual of Housekeeping*. n.p.: Penguin Books in association with the National Trust, 1984. Sensible advice on the care of books along with all the other objects that might be found in old houses.

Thomson, Garry. *The Museum Environment*, 2nd ed., London: Butterworths, 1986. This is written for conservators, but the first half is clearly stated and interesting for the layman.

Waters, Peter. *Procedures for Salvage of Water-damaged Library Materials*. Washington: Library of Congress, 1975. A revised edition of this classic handbook is now available.

Collecting.

Carter, John. *ABC for Book Collectors*, 6th rev. ed., London: Granada, 1985. This is full of useful information and also very amusing.

Collins, L. A. *Collecting books in New England, An introduction for the Beginning Collector and the Home Library Builder, With Directories of Used Book Shops and Annual Used Book Sales*. West Lebanon, ME: Robert J. Diefendorf, 1983. No comment other than the title is needed.

Muir, P. H. *Book-collecting as a Hobby, In a Series of Letters to Everyman*. New York: Alfred A. Knopf, 1947. A leisurely, pleasant book with good advice in it.

Peters, Jean. *Book Collecting: A Modern Guide*. New York: R. R. Bowker, 1977. A manual for the beginning collector. See particularly "The Literature of Book Collecting" by G. Thomas Tanselle.

———. *Collectible Books: Some New Paths*. New York: R. R. Bowker, 1979. Not so new now, but still an important book on various aspects of collecting.

Sheppard, Roger and Judith. *International Directory of Book Collectors, A directory of antiquarian and secondhand book dealers in the U.S.A. and Canada, 1986–87*, 10th ed., London: Europa Publications, 1987. Uniform with this volume are: *Dealers in Books* (British Isles), *European Bookdealers*, *Bookdealers in India*.

Thomas, Alan G. *Great books and book collectors*. New York: Excalibur Books, 1983. Discursive and very pleasant reading.

Wilson, Robert A. *Modern Book Collecting*, New York: Alfred A. Knopf, 1980. An introduction to collecting early twentieth century American and English literature.

History and Reference

The following list is restricted to a few general works. Most of these books are profusely illustrated.

Blumenthal, Joseph. *Art of the printed book, 1455–1955, Masterpieces of Typography throughout five centuries from the collections of the*

Pierpont Morgan Library, New York. New York: The Pierpont Morgan Library, 1973.

Breslauer, B. H. *The Uses of Bookbinding Literature*. New York: Book Arts Press, 1986. A brief, informative outline of the subject. Available from the School of Library Service, Columbia University.

Breslauer, Martin. *Fine books in fine bindings from the fourteenth to the present century*, Catalogue 104 and 104:II. New York: Breslauer, Inc., n.d. Learned, sumptuous catalogs, very profusely illustrated.

Cockerell, Douglas. *Bookbinding and the care of books*, 5th ed., London: Pitman, 1971. This is a classic 'hands-on' book on binding. Cockerell reformed hand bookbinding practices early in this century.

de Hamel, Christopher. *A History of Illuminated Manuscripts*. Oxford: Phaidon, 1986.

Devauchelle, R. *La reliure en France de ses origines à nos jours*. Paris: J. Rousseau-Girard, 1959–1961.

French, Hannah D. *Bookbinding in early America*, Worcester, MA: American Antiquarian Society, 1986.

Gaskell, Philip. *A New Introduction to Bibliography*. Oxford: New York and Oxford: Oxford University Press, 1972. Covers the processes of hand book production from 1500 to 1800. Annotated bibliography.

Gilissen, Léon. *La reliure occidental antérieure à 1400*. Turnhout: Brepols, 1983. The emphasis is on binding structure with examples from the Royal Library in Brussels. Excellent photographs.

Glaister, Geoffrey A. *Glaister's Glossary of the Book*, 2nd rev. ed., Berkeley: University of California Press, 1979.

Goldschmidt, E. P. *Gothic and Renaissance bookbindings*, 2 v., London: Ernest Benn Ltd, 1928.

Hindeman, Sandra and James D. Farquhar. *Pen to Press, Illustrated Manuscripts and Printed Books in the First Century of Printing*. n.p.: University of Maryland, John Hopkins, 1977.

Lawson, Alexander. *Printing types, An Introduction*. Boston: Beacon Press, 1971.

Lehmann-Haupt, Hellmut, ed. *Bookbinding in America, Three essays*. New York: R. R. Bowker Co., reprinted 1967. The three essays are: "Early American Bookbinding by Hand" by Hannah Dustin French; "The Rise of American Edition Binding" by Joseph W. Rogers; "On the Rebinding of Old Books" by Hellmut Lemann-Haupt.

Maggs Bros. Ltd. *Bookbinding in Great Britain, Sixteenth to the Twentieth Century*, Catalog 893 (1964); 966 (1975); 1014 (1981). *Bookbinding in the British Iles*, Catalog 1075, 2v. (1987). These catalogs are very informative with numerous illustrations.

Middleton, Bernard C. *A History of English Craft Bookbinding Technique*, 2nd supplemented ed., New York and London: Hafner Publishing Co., 1978. One of the very few books on structure described in the order of the steps in binding.

Miner, Dorothy, *The History of bookbinding, 525–1950 A.D.* Baltimore: Trustees of the Walters Art Gallery, 1957. This is an excellent general survey of binding history. Many illustrations.

Needham, Paul. *Twelve Centuries of Bookbindings, 400–1600*. New York: The Pierpont Morgan Library, 1979.

Papermaking: art and craft. Washington: Library of Congress, 1968. An excellent survey, available from the Library of Congress.

Regemorter, Berthe van, "The bound codex from its origin to the early Middle Ages," translated by Mary E. [Jane] Greenfield, Guild of Book Workers *Journal* 17:1,2,3 (1978–79) 1–25.

Roberts, C. H. and T. C. Skeat. *The Birth of the Codex*. London: Oxford University Press, 1983.

Roberts, Matt T. and Don Etherington. *Bookbinding and the Conservation of Books, A diction-*

ary of descriptive terminology. Washington: Library of Congress, 1982.

Shailor, Barbara A. *The Medieval Book, Catalogue of an Exhibition at the Beinecke Rare Book and Manuscript Library, Yale University* New Haven, CT, 1988.

Spawn, Willman. *Bookbinding in America, 1680–1910*. Bryn Mawr, PA: Bryn Mawr College Library, 1983.

———. "Identifying eighteenth century American bookbinders," Guild of Book Workers *Journal* 17:1,2,3 (1978–79) 25–37.

Thomas, Isiah. *The History of Printing in America, with a Biography of Printers and an Account of Newspapers*. New York: Weathervane Books, 1970. Originally published in 1810. Thomas was a printer himself and knew many of the printers he wrote about.

Wroth, L. C. *The Colonial Printer*, 2nd rev. ed. Portland, ME: The Southworth-Anthoensen Press, 1938.

Periodicals

The Abbey Newsletter, Bookbinding and conservation
320 East Center Street
Provo, Utah 84601
(801)373–1598
This is published six or more times a year. It contains current information on bookbinding and conservation, products and services, publications, coming events, etc.

Alkaline Paper Advocate
A new publication, estimated publication schedule four or five times a year. Publisher: Abbey Publications with the same address as the Abbey Newsletter.

The Book Collector
The Collector Ltd.
90 Great Russell Street
London WC1B 3PY
England
Published four times a year. Contains articles on bibliography, collecting, binding and printing.
Telephone: 01–637–3029

Paper Conservation News
The Institute of Paper Conservation
Leigh Lodge
Leigh
Worcester WR6 5LB
England
Published four times a year. It contains current information on paper, conservation, bookbinding, products and services, publications, coming events, etc.

Restaurator
Munksgaard International Publishers
535 Norre Sogade
DK-1370 Copenhagen
Denmark
Published irregularly. Contains articles on the preservation of library materials.

Index

Index